With the 'Trotting Twelfth'

With the 'Trotting Twelfth'

The Recollections of a Private &
Quartermaster-Sergeant of the 12th Rhode
Island Volunteers During the American Civil War

My First Campaign

J. W. Grant

Reminiscences of Service with the Twelfth
Rhode Island Volunteers

Pardon E. Tillinghast

LEONAUR

With the 'Trotting Twelfth'
The Recollections of a Private & Quartermaster-Sergeant of the 12th Rhode
Island Volunteers During the American Civil War
My First Campaign
by J. W. Grant
Reminiscences of Service with the Twelfth Rhode Island Volunteers
by Pardon E. Tillinghast

First published under the titles
My First Campaign
and
Reminiscences of Service with the Twelfth Rhode Island Volunteers,
and a Memorial of Col. George H. Browne.

Leonaur is an imprint of Oakpast Ltd

Copyright in this form © 2011 Oakpast Ltd

ISBN: 978-0-85706-657-2 (hardcover)
ISBN: 978-0-85706-658-9 (softcover)

http://www.leonaur.com

Publisher's Notes

The opinions of the authors represent a view of events in which he
was a participant related from his own perspective,
as such the text is relevant as an historical document.

The views expressed in this book are not necessarily
those of the publisher.

Contents

My First Campaign

J. W. Grant

Contents

Preface

At the earnest request of many of my comrades of the Twelfth Rhode Island Volunteers, I am induced to publish this narrative, which, with very little addition or alteration, I have copied entire from my private journal. This was written under many disadvantages during a campaign of unusual hardships and privations. Hoping it may prove of use, as a reference, to many of my companions, who from the very nature of the campaign, found it impossible to keep a record, is the only apology I have to offer for publishing a work of this nature.

Diamond Hill, R. I., August, 1863.

Chapter 1

The Volunteer

On the 16th day of September, 1862, the author of this narrative was duly enlisted as a volunteer in the service of the United States; and, on the 22nd of the same month, reported at Camp Stevens, Providence, R. I., for duty. At this place, the Twelfth Regiment Rhode Island Volunteers was organized; and in this city, on the 13th day of October, 1862, it was mustered into the service of the United States, for a period of nine months.

As a member of this regiment, your subscriber was duly elected, and from the 13th of October, 1862, until the 29th of July, 1863, was known as J. W. Grant, private, Company F, Twelfth Regiment Rhode Island Volunteers. Our regiment was under the command of Colonel George H. Browne, and as yet no lieutenant-colonel or major had been assigned us. The following were the company officers:

Company A.—Captain, Edward S. Cheney; 1st Lieutenant, ——; 2nd Lieutenant, John S. Roberts.

Company B.—Captain, James M. Longstreet; 1st Lieutenant, Oscar Lapham; 2nd Lieutenant, Albert W. Delanah.

Company C.—Captain, James H. Allen; 1st Lieutenant, Jales Macharet; 2nd Lieutenant, Matthew M. Chappell.

Company D.—Captain, George C. Almy; 1st Lieutenant, William H. King; 2nd Lieutenant, George H. Tabor.

Company E.—Captain, John J. Phillips; 1st Lieutenant, George F. Bicknell; 2nd Lieutenant, Christopher H. Alexander.

Company F.—Captain, William E. Hubbard; 1st Lieutenant, George F. Lawton; 2nd Lieutenant, George Bucklin.

Company G.—Captain, ——; 1st Lieutenant, William C. Rogers; 2nd Lieutenant, James Bowen.

Company H.—Captain, Oliver H. Perry; 1st Lieutenant, ——; 2nd Lieutenant, Edward P. Butts, Jr.

Company I.—Captain, George A. Spink; 1st Lieutenant, Stephen M. Hopkins; 2nd Lieutenant, Munson H. Najac.

Company K.—Captain, ——; 1st Lieutenant, Edmund W. Fales; 2nd Lieutenant, James M. Pendleton.

John L. Clark, of Cumberland, was appointed Quartermaster, and John Turner, of Bristol, Adjutant.

On the 21st day of October, at six o'clock, p.m., the Twelfth Rhode Island Volunteers formed for its last parade, on Camp Stevens, and at seven, p.m., of the same day we were aboard the cars, and hurrying on our way *en route* for Washington, by way of New York and Baltimore.

We reached Groton at half-past nine, went aboard the steamer *Plymouth Rock* at this place, and at eleven were moving down the Sound.

It was rather an unpleasant night; the wind blew fresh from the south, rolling up the clouds in heavy masses, with every appearance of its raining immediately. However, at daybreak, the wind changed to the north-west, the clouds began to disperse, and at sunrise the sky was perfectly clear.

Just beyond Hurl Gate we passed the steamer *Great Eastern* lying at anchor, and had as good a view of her as we could desire to have. She appears to be a beautifully modelled vessel, of tremendous size and power.

We arrived in Jersey City at eight, a.m. Disembarking from the *Plymouth Rock*, we re-embarked on the steamer *Kill Von Hull*, and at ten, a.m., were steaming towards Elizabethport, the wind blowing a gale, dead ahead. Passed by Staten Island, which by the way is one of the most beautiful places I have ever seen. The land rises from the bay to a very great height, and is covered with groves of beautiful trees, interspersed with houses here and there. I should think, from the appearance of Staten Island, that it must be a delightful place.

As we sailed along, close by the shore, the people came from the houses to salute us, waving flags and handkerchiefs; in the groves and upon the house-tops we saw and heard them cheering us. We arrived at Elizabethport about twelve o'clock. I should think it to be a place of some importance as a depot for the shipment of coal, there being every convenience in the line of railways and wharfs. It is a small place, however, nothing doing except in connection with the coal trade. We started from this place at three, p.m., *en route* for Baltimore, by way of Harrisburg.

The soil at Elizabethport, and all the way through New Jersey, by rail to Phillipsburg, Penn., is a reddish brown clay, and for the first twenty-five miles beyond Elizabethport the country appears quite monotonous, a vast level plain, with here and there a shrub, and a few houses, but no good farms. The only fruit trees I saw worth mentioning were quinces; these were of large size, and many of them were loaded down with fruit. I should suppose this road ran through the most barren part of Jersey, as I could see no signs of thrift and industry.

Upon entering Phillipsburg we came upon a most beautiful country, abounding in hills and valleys, covered with forest trees, with here and there an excellent farm. The hills are high and smooth—no rocks to be seen upon the surface—thereby affording some of the finest situations for farming I ever saw. The scenery is most beautiful all the way through Pennsylvania on this line. In consequence of the unevenness of the surface through this part of the country, the railroad cuts are very frequent and extensive, some of them extending for a mile or more, and so deep that we could hardly see the top of the bank from the car window. The road, also, of necessity crosses ravines, some of them one hundred and fifty feet in depth.

We arrived at Phillipsburg at five o'clock, p.m.; halted the trains, filled canteens, and relieved four or five apple trees of two or three bushels of fruit. Stopped at Phillipsburg until after dark, to allow trains of coal to pass, this being the great thoroughfare over which vast quantities of coal pass to Elizabethport, from the coal districts of Pennsylvania. After starting from Phillipsburg we moved along very slow, stopping often, and passing frequently tremendous long trains of coal, drawn by powerful locomotives, two locomotives attached to many of the trains.

We arrived at Easton at nine o'clock Wednesday evening. Here I saw canal boats running for the first time, passing and repassing one another, and learned we were upon the Schuylkill River,—and crossed this beautiful stream immediately after leaving this place.

After leaving Easton, we slept in the cars, as well as we could. Passed through Reading in the night, and the next morning found ourselves close by, and at sunrise entered Harrisburg, the capital of Pennsylvania. It is not a very large place, but it is pleasantly situated, the neighbourhood abounding in beautiful scenery. Stopped at this place, got out of the cars, crossed the canal, and formed in line; called the roll in the streets of Harrisburg, went immediately aboard of the cars again,—and, after a series of running ahead and backs, into and out of the depot, finally started, changing direction for Baltimore. The bridge crossing the Susquehanna at this place is a very fine structure; I should think it to be nearly a mile in length, and crosses the river at a height of nearly seventy feet above the surface of the water.

The road lay close by the river for a long distance, affording us a fine view of this celebrated stream. I looked forward, with a great deal of interest, to the time of crossing the line into Maryland, expecting to see quite a change in the looks of things upon entering a slave state, judging from what I had heard. We crossed the line about twelve o'clock, and I found myself agreeably disappointed in the appearance of things. Instead of seeing an abundance of negroes I hardly saw one. The houses are small and cheaply built, most of them, as they are indeed all the way from New York, but I could see no difference in the people; all I saw, on the whole route from New York, were not as well dressed, or as neat in appearance as they are in New England.

The scenery, all the way to Baltimore, continued to be most beautiful, and the country appears to be well adapted, in all respects, to farming operations. I saw quite extensive fields of corn in Maryland and Pennsylvania; the corn was being carried outside of the fields, to be husked there, most of it, I should think, as I saw men busy in many places stripping off the husks and carrying it away. They manage to get their corn off in time to sow the same piece to grain. Several of the fields were already cleared of the corn, the grains sown and already up two and three inches high. There seems to a New Englander a great lack of barns and other outbuildings in these States, but with the crops they raise perhaps they are not necessary.

We journeyed along very slow after leaving Harrisburg, stopping often for wood and water, also for trains to pass by us, &c. The road we found to be strictly guarded, long before we came to Baltimore, passing company after company on picket duty along the road, who cheered as we went past. Feeling our way along, we came into Baltimore just at dark, Thursday evening, the 23rd. Got out of the cars, the regiment was formed, and we proceeded through the streets of this city to our resting place for the night. Halted at the general rendezvous for soldiers long enough to take refreshments; sat down, unslung knapsacks, and commenced our supper, which consisted of coffee, white bread, beef, ham, tongue, *sour krout*, &c.

Slung knapsacks, went from there to the depot, unslung knapsacks again, and camped for the night upon the depot floor. Drums beat at six o'clock, a.m., the 24th, for roll call; tumbled out of *bed*—the regiment was formed, and we went to breakfast, at the same place where we took supper the night before, which was but a short distance from the depot. After breakfast we marched back, formed in line in front of the depot; rested there until ten o'clock, then marched through the principal streets of the city; visited Washington Monument, a beautiful structure of white marble, surmounted by a statue of the *Great Chieftain*. Halted to rest around the base; then marched back, visiting the monument erected to the memory of those who fell at Fort McHenry in 1812, and formed in line where we started from, to wait and take the cars for Washington. Baltimore is indeed a fine place—no wonder the rebels envy us the possession of it. I saw some splendid buildings in the Monumental city.

We finally got aboard of the cars, and started for Washington, at five, p.m. Just before dark passed the "Relay Station," where the Massachusetts Eighth were encamped in 1861. Passed picket after picket, guarding the road, their camp fires burning, lighting us up as we passed along, and finally reached the great capital, at eleven, p.m. We proceeded immediately to our quarters, unslung knapsacks, then marched about forty rods to the "Soldiers' Retreat," where we took supper; then marched to our quarters, and at one o'clock, a.m., turned in. At half-past six we arose to look about us. It was indeed a pleasant morning, the sun was shining brightly, and everything betokened a pleasant day.

The first object that struck my eye was the Capitol, not more than quarter of a mile distant. It is yet unfinished, but nearer completion than I supposed it to be from what I had heard. At nine, a.m., with a few others, I went inside; stopped in the rotunda a while, to look at the paintings, and then passed up a flight of marble steps leading into the right wing of the building, to get a view of the House of Representatives. We passed through entries, and by reception rooms, the floors of which were of "stone mosaic," looking to all appearances like beautiful carpeting. The ceiling overhead was supported by marble pillars of exquisite design and finish, situated just inside of niches in the walls. The "House of Representatives" is a magnificent room, entirely beyond my powers of description.

From thence we proceeded to the rotunda, and entered the left wing of the building by a flight of stairs, corresponding with those we had just left, the style of finish being the same along the whole passage as of that leading to the House, in the other wing. This passage leads to the "Senate Chamber." This room is somewhat different from that of the House, but rather plainer in its general appearance. The pillars supporting the galleries and ceiling are very numerous, of Egyptian marble, or something similar in appearance. The walls and arches overhead are covered with fresco paintings, of great beauty and variety. We had but a short time allowed us to visit this place, and consequently did not see but a small portion of it.

I had understood, that apart from the Capitol, the city was a miserable looking place. I do not see it in that light. There is certainly a great deal to do—a great deal yet unfinished—but it is certainly more of a place than it has been represented to be. A few years more and this will be a beautiful city; the present war already begins to tell upon it. The business doing here necessarily in carrying on this war is creating a stimulus; buildings are going up, improvements are being made, and men of real business talent are encouraged to come here. The ball is set in motion, and this place, in a few years, will present a far different appearance from what it does at the present time.

I was hoping we might stop in Washington two or three days, but was disappointed. At eleven o'clock Saturday, the 25th, we formed in line, passed in front of the Capitol, down Pennsylvania Avenue, turned off to the right in the direction of Long Bridge, passed Washington Monument, leaving it to the left of us, and forming in line opposite General Casey's headquarters, to whose division we were assigned, gave him three hearty cheers, and at twelve o'clock passed on to Long Bridge, and into *Dixie*.

The Potomac is very broad and shallow at this place, except in the channel. It has the appearance of the flats on the sea coast, the water being but about six inches or a foot deep at the time of our crossing, showing a smooth, muddy bottom, covered with weeds, &c. After crossing, we proceeded about a mile up a hill, and came to a halt upon a plain. It was quite a warm, dusty day, and a rest at this time was very acceptable to us. Stopped half an hour, started again, proceeded about a mile farther, filed to the right, and forming our camp upon an eminence within sight of the dome of the Capitol, we pitched our tents, Saturday night, just in time to shelter us from the rain, which the next day (Sunday the 26th) commenced pouring in torrents, and continued through the day and night.

We had twenty-two in our tent Sunday night; two of them slept immediately in the centre of the tent, just under the "cap." This "cap" is a circular piece of cloth (peculiar to the "Sibley Tent") ingeniously contrived for the purpose of ventilation; it is easily moved by means of ropes which hang upon the outside, and the aperture which it covers can be made larger or smaller, at the pleasure of the occupants. As it happened it blew a gale in the night, and the "cap" not being properly fastened on, blew off, and the rain came down upon T——n and J——s, who turned out in the morning in rather a dilapidated condition.

Monday the 27th the storm blew over; at noon the sun came out; we dried our blankets, and Tuesday, the 28th, re-pitched our tents in regular order.

Sunday, November 2nd, we received orders to move. Packed knapsacks, and at eleven, a.m., bade farewell to "Camp Chase," filed out into the road, and turning to the right, passed on up a hill, and continued on in the direction of Fairfax. Passed the Seminary buildings at twelve, m. These buildings, so often spoken of in connection with this rebellion, are built of brick, with some pretension to beauty in their architecture; connected with the main building is a fine looking tower, from the summit of which the country can be seen for many miles around. Upon an eminence, and almost hidden from view by the thick grove of trees surrounding them, they stand objects of interest to all acquainted with the history of this war. Six miles to the north of here, and partly in view, is the capital, from which place the course of the Potomac can be discerned for many miles, as it bears away to the south and east of us.

Leaving this place we descended a hill, and passed the Common, which is a short distance south-east of the Seminary. This Common is now used as a burial place for soldiers. Each grave has a neat wooden slab, with the name of the deceased, the regiment and company to which he belonged painted upon it.

Continuing along one-half a mile farther, we filed to the right up a steep hill, and at two, p.m., formed our camp again, and pitched our tents upon the top of it, on a level space directly between two large houses, the owners of which are now in the rebel army, having left this beautiful situation to be occupied by our troops, and their houses to be used as hospitals, for the comfort of our sick and wounded soldiers.

The road from "Fairfax Seminary" passed along close by, on the side of the hill, our camp facing it towards the east. The city of Alexandria is one and a half miles to the east of us, and partly in view. The great highway from Alexandria to "Fairfax Court House," and Manassas, passed our camp, running east and west, not more than fifty rods south of us, at right angles with the road passing from the north, and connecting with it. This road was lined with ambulances, baggage wagons, &c., going to and from Alexandria, Fairfax Court House and Manassas, in the vicinity of which a portion of our army were at that time encamped. The railroad from Alexandria to Manassas was half a mile to the south of us in the valley, and ran parallel with the wagon road for two miles—then bore away farther to the south, as it rose the hills beyond. The trains were running night and day, carrying reinforcements and stores to our army.

These roads were in full view of our camp for three or four miles. We could see the trains as they started from Alexandria, and could watch them as they continue their journey far to the west of us. The level space on the top of this hill covers an area of perhaps six or seven acres, of an irregular shape. Our tents were pitched upon the southern point, and those of another regiment upon the northern part of the space, at an elevation of perhaps two hundred feet above the level of the Potomac, which flows along in full view of us.

Across a deep valley to the north-west, and perhaps half a mile distant, was Fort Worth, and to the south of this fort, upon the wagon road, were "Cloud's Mills," so often spoken of during this rebellion.

The descent of the hill, towards the south and west was very steep. Its side was covered with springs, which afforded us plenty of water; and at the bottom of the valley, to the west, was a fine stream, running towards the south, originating in a spring at the foot of the hill, south of the Seminary buildings. The Seminary, Fort Worth, and our camp, were all on about the same elevation, forming half of a circle—the Seminary at the north, our camp on the south-eastern, and Fort Worth on the south-western point. Taking into consideration the surroundings and associations connected with the situation, I think we could not have chosen a more pleasant or interesting place for our camp.

Monday, November 3rd, the next day after forming our camp, we packed haversacks, and had our first experience in picket duty, our Company and Company G being detailed for that purpose. At half-past eight we filed down the hill, turned to the right, on the road to Manassas; passed "Cloud's Mills" at nine, a.m., and continued on as far as "Bailey's Cross Roads," a place become familiar to us all in the history of this war. At this place we stopped, and fixed our quarters; posting our pickets along the road. We were fortunate in having pleasant weather while we were upon this duty.

The next day, at eleven, a.m., the reserve formed in line to receive the "New Guard," and at twelve o'clock we started for camp. Stopped when within half a mile, and discharged our pieces, which were heavily loaded with ball and buckshot, and at two, p.m., arrived again in camp, bringing in two prisoners, who by the way, however, proved to be loyal soldiers, without passes.

Our camp was named "Camp Casey, near Fairfax Seminary," and we, with three other regiments, were encamped close to one other, formerly the first brigade of General Casey's Division, commanded by Colonel Wright, acting Brigadier-General. Our regiment was engaged in drilling, doing fatigue, picket and guard duty, which kept us busy. Fifty of our regiment were detailed November 7th to do fatigue duty in Fort Blenker, digging, shovelling, &c. The boys going out, came in at ten, a.m., driven in by the storm which was raging there. It commenced storming the 6th, and at ten, a.m., the next day it had culminated into an old-fashioned New England snow storm. The wind blew a gale; the air was very cold, and the snow, whirling about us, made our situation very uncomfortable, especially to those who were on guard, and exposed to its fury. B. was the only one from D. H. happening to be on guard, except W. S., who volunteered to take another man's place for $1.25. I think he earned his money.

Chapter 2

Learning Our Trade

The snow storm of November 7th came upon us quite un-expectedly, leading us to think we had journeyed in the wrong direction, and instead of being in "Dixie" had approached the north pole, and were already in the immediate vicinity of it. There were some wry faces about the camp, though most seemed amused at this unlooked-for event, joking among themselves at the idea of making snowballs in Virginia before Rhode Islanders could get the necessary material—"enlisting under false pre-tences," &c.

From November 8th to the 12th, nothing of unusual interest occurred, our time being taken up in drill, and in other necessary duties connected with camp-life. November 13th, the entire regiment was ordered to be in readiness the following morning, for picket duty, with two days' rations. The appearance of the sky, the night of the 12th, was threatening, making us already feel, in imagination, the discomforts of this duty in a storm, with no other shelter but the broad canopy of the heavens, excepting, perhaps, a paltry one of bushes, affording indeed but little pro-tection from the pitiless storm.

The morning of the 13th came; the roll of drums at six o'clock, aroused many a drowsy soldier of the Twelfth from his humble couch, and interrupted many a pleasant dream of home, to awake him to the stern reality of other duties and associations. It did, indeed, rain in the night, which proved a benefit to us, raining just enough to lay the dust. The morning broke upon us with the assurance of a pleasant day. With cheerful hearts and willing hands, we began our preparations. We took breakfast at the usual hour, half-past seven, filled our haversacks with beef and hard crackers, our canteens with water, strapped our blankets about us, buckled on our equipments, and at eight o'clock, formed in line in the Company Street, and at half-past eight, the different companies passed Gen. Wright's headquarters.

The regiment was formed for "guard-mounting," directly in front of his residence, went through the manoeuvres, listened to the music from the Brigade Band, (which, by the way, discoursed finely,) and at quarter to nine, filed into the road, and taking the direction of Fairfax Court House, were fairly on our way. Everything was favourable; a cool breeze from the northwest, adding to our comfort, as we "marched along." We were accompanied by nearly all our officers, a few being left behind, as is customary, to protect our camp. After passing Cloud's Mills, and ascending the hill beyond, we came to a halt, and the regiment was divided into parties of 108 privates, each division to be commanded by their respective officers. These divisions are called "supports," and numbered first, second, third, &c.

As soon as our "support" was formed, we continued our march. Passed the road leading to Bailey's Cross Roads, kept along on the direct road to Fairfax Court House, for about a mile beyond this turn, then filing to the left, entered the woods, followed a cart-path for about half a mile, and at eleven, a.m., found ourselves at the end of our journey. There were plenty of good shelters where we were to encamp, already erected by those there before us, and gladly vacated by the Twenty-Seventh New Jersey, who turned out to receive us upon our arrival.

Our "support" was immediately divided into three "reliefs," of 36 men each. Each "relief" to stay on four hours, the first going on to be relieved by the second, &c., giving each "relief" eight hours rest at the general rendezvous. The "reliefs" were arranged in two ranks, and numbered as they stood, from right to left, each man to remember the number assigned him, and when called upon, place himself in the ranks accordingly. I found myself in the first "relief," number 21, armed and equipped as the law directs.

As soon as our "relief" was formed, we started for our posts, marched back to the road we had just left, continued on half a mile farther, and came upon Post No. 1. This post was on the main road, and close by the ruins of what was once a large building, destroyed, probably, since the war commenced, nothing being left now but a mass of brick and stone. Upon relieving this post, we left the road, which here runs nearly east and west, and struck across the fields towards the south, for Post No. 2.

The posts were perhaps thirty rods apart; three men being stationed on each post, and one sergeant or corporal, in charge of every three posts. The first three men, as numbered in the ranks before starting from the rendezvous, to take the first post, the next three the second, &c. The orders were for one man to remain at the post, while the other two were to move to and from the post, in opposite directions, a certain distance, or perhaps farther, occasionally, if the sentinel from the posts adjoining, should fail to meet him at the end of his beat, thereby keeping up communication throughout the entire line. The men to have their pieces loaded, and bayonets fixed, with particular instructions to be on the alert, to build no fires, light no matches, smoke, nor indulge in loud conversation.

The line of pickets ran nearly north and south, the first "support" being on the right of the line, commenced in the vicinity of Bailey's Cross Roads, and connected with the second "support," at Post No. 1. The line of our "support" ran from the main road, towards the railroad, the distance between the two, at this place, being perhaps one and a half miles, our "support" reaching two-thirds of the way to the railroad, there to connect with the third, and so on to the last "support," our regiment guarding a line of several miles in length. Our path led over level spaces, up and down hills steep as the roof of a house, alongside hills where it required the greatest care to preserve our equilibrium, through tangled thickets of bush and brier, and over every conceivable obstacle in the shape of stump, stone, bog, &c.

26

The place falling to my lot, to help guard for the next forty-eight hours, was Post No. 7, just in the edge of a grove of small evergreen trees, on the side of a hill, overlooking what must have been once a large farm, situated in a valley opening to the south, and enclosed on three sides by woods. Our post was on the eastern side of this clearing; the hill on the opposite side, rising to about the same height, was covered with a heavy growth of timber, affording a good shelter for sharpshooters, if they had happened to have been in the vicinity, and had been disposed to annoy us. The distance across this clearing being about one-third of a mile, a good distance for rifle practice.

This clearing was perhaps fifty rods in width, and nearly one-third of a mile in length, bounded on the north by a swamp, and opening to the south upon a vast plain of bog, with here and there a bunch of stunted trees or bushes. Quite a large stream issues from this swamp, and runs the entire length of the farm, emptying into a larger one, which runs into the Potomac, along the valley through which the railroad runs from Alexandria to Manassas. The ruins of a large farmhouse lay in the valley to the left of us. I will not omit a description of the "beat" over which your humble servant kept watch and ward, until every foot of ground became familiar to him.

The path alongside this clearing had been lately cut through, without much regard to convenience of travelling, or risk of life or limb, the stumps sticking up invariably from three to six inches from the ground, requiring the utmost care on our part, especially in the night time, or the privilege of trying, if we chose, the sharpness of these stubs, upon various parts of our body, or the hardness of our heads against the trees by the way-side, experiments in tripping and plunging not likely to find favour with your humble servant.

We were very fortunate in having pleasant weather again for this duty. We took our posts at twelve, unslung our blankets, haversacks and canteens, and loaded our pieces. We were relieved at four o'clock, and arrived at the rendezvous in time to make our coffee before dark, eat our supper, spread our blankets and turn in.

Slept soundly, and at midnight, when we were again called upon, marched to our posts, to remain there till four o'clock. The night was warm and pleasant; the moon was just rising as we took our posts, which made our duty much easier; our four hours passed quickly by, we were relieved again, and at half-past four were again at the rendezvous. We had anticipated having another nap before breakfast, and were getting ready to turn in, when we were ordered to form in line and stand until sunrise. Our colonel represented it as necessary, to guard against surprise; as the enemy usually make attacks at this hour—a watchfulness much to be commended, in the vicinity of the enemy, but as our picket was of importance only as a guard to intercept deserters and stragglers from our army in front, we, with our sleepy eyes, could not see the *point*.

Many of the men, without much deference to the opinion of our brave colonel, thought it simply ridiculous; some cursed, others laughed and joked. I did not regret losing my nap, as I was amply repaid, listening to the witticisms of the party. Morning broke at last, and we were relieved. We kindled our fires anew, made our coffee, and after breakfast some of us turned in to sleep; others played cards, or amused themselves as they chose, until twelve, when we took our posts again. The weather continued fine, and we passed the time pleasantly.

Another night passed; another pleasant day opened upon us, nothing remarkable occurring in connection with our duties, unless we except a visit from General Casey, who rode along the line, accompanied by his staff, on a tour of inspection. At eleven o'clock, a.m., the 15th, we formed in line to receive the new guard, and by twelve our last relief was in, and we started for camp. We reached it about two, p.m., all of us in good spirits; found our dinner of soup and hot coffee waiting for us, to which we immediately paid our respects.

The next morning, Sunday, the 16th, we cleaned our muskets, brushed our clothes, and at eleven, a.m., attended divine service, the chaplain holding forth from the steps of the building which adjoins our camp on the north, the regiment forming on the lawn in front. This building is very large, and is now used by the colonel, he taking up his quarters there, the post-office, hospital and quartermaster's department being included in the same building; giving our field and staff plenty of room and good accommodations.

Monday, the 17th, was not as pleasant; quite a strong wind from the south-west, cloudy and misty, making it rather hard to turn out and drill. Tuesday, the 18th, was a complete pattern of the 17th; a thick fog, just enough to make it unpleasant; drilled through the day, however, and at dress parade had orders to be in readiness the following morning to march to Fort Albany, to be reviewed by General Casey.

The wind continued blowing strong from the south through the night, and the next morning the black, heavy clouds rolling up, showed certain signs of a wet day. At eight o'clock the company formed in the street, marched on to the parade ground; the regiment was formed, and at half-past eight filed into the road and started on our journey. Stopped opposite General Wright's headquarters for the other regiments to take their place in line, it being a review of the whole brigade.

At quarter before nine the Fifth Connecticut came in ahead, the Thirteenth New Hampshire formed in the rear, and we started on. After proceeding two miles, the order was counter-manded, and we hurried back just in time to escape a drenching rain, which poured in torrents immediately after our arrival in camp. The government having furnished us with stoves, and plenty of wood, we kept our tents, and contrived to make ourselves comfortable.

The next day, the 21st, our turn came for picket duty again. One of the regiments belonging to our brigade, the Twenty-Seventh New Jersey, having been taken from us, our turn came two days sooner than we had anticipated it would, when on before. It continued raining throughout the afternoon, and towards night the wind, which had been blowing from the south, came round into the north-east, much against our wishes; and it continued raining through the night. In the morning we found the wind had hauled into the north, the rain had nearly ceased, and at eight o'clock our regiment were in line; and at half-past eight were on their march.

By eleven, a.m., the sky was clear, and the Twelfth Rhode Island Volunteers were again favoured with pleasant weather. While the other regiments of our brigade had to contend with storms and unpleasant weather, while on this picket duty, the Twelfth thus far escaped. Having some work of my own to do, I stopped in camp this time, and did not accompany the regiment. Saturday, the 22nd, it was very warm and pleasant; but Sunday, the 23rd, the sky was partially overcast with clouds, the air was raw and chilly, and the wind blew a gale from the north-west.

At two o'clock, p.m., our regiment came in, all in good spirits, but glad to get into camp. Monday, 24th, we had a pleasant day again, and a fine time drilling. The mud had dried up, the ground had become hard, there was no dust blowing, and the men were in fine spirits, and fast improving in the drill and discipline necessary to make the soldier.

The Twelfth as yet continued to be in remarkably good health, compared with the other regiments encamped about us. The Thirteenth New Hampshire and Fifth Connecticut, coming here at the same time with us, had already lost several men since encamping here, and had then quite a number sick in the hospital. Our fare continued good; we had excellent bread, and plenty of it. It was baked at Alexandria, and we got it fresh, and oftentimes warm from the oven. We had hard crackers occasionally, twice a week, perhaps, instead of soft bread. The hard bread we had here was entirely different from what I expected to find it. It appeared to be made of the best of material.

Our salt beef was fat, of good quality, and when properly cooked, was as good as we could ask for. It is cured differently from that at home, there being much saltpetre used in curing it; requiring a great deal of pains, on the part of the cooks, in order to make it palatable. We had fresh beef twice a week; this was made into soups. Our company finally procured a large sheet iron pan, six feet long and two feet in width, to be used as a frying-pan, and after that we had fried beef once or twice a week. We had tea or coffee twice a day, (with our breakfast and supper,) with plenty of sugar to accompany it. We had rice, and sugar-house syrup, bean soup, &c. Anyone finding fault with our fare at this time would be apt to be dissatisfied wherever he were placed.

Tuesday, 25th, was a cloudy, misty day, and in the night it rained quite hard. Wednesday morning it cleared off in time for us to drill. It had rained just enough to soften the clay, the mud being shallow and as slippery as grease—a peculiarity in the mud about here. You can appreciate this kind of travelling by spreading lard an inch thick upon a plank, and then attempting to walk upon it. One advantage in this kind of soil is that when it dries it becomes as hard as a cement floor, which made it easier for us than to have been wallowing through sand. The weather continued pleasant, no dust blowing about and into everything; the ground was hard, in the best condition for drilling, and our regiment improved it.

The 27th was Thanksgiving Day in Rhode Island, and also duly observed by us in camp. We were relieved from drill, attended divine service at eleven, a.m., and had a little recreation, walking about the country, &c. Our bed-sacks were now given out to us, with plenty of clean straw to fill them with. (These sacks were made of stout ticking, and were, perhaps, seven feet long and five feet wide, after they were filled; amply large enough, each of them, for two to lie upon.) The regiment were all provided with these sacks, and had lain upon the ground long enough to know how to appreciate them. The 27th was a beautiful day, and having never been to Alexandria, I took this opportunity to visit the place.

Procured a pass, and in company with one of our mess, at eight, a.m., started. We struck a "bee line" directly for the place; passed over the road leading from Fairfax Seminary, and continued on, uphill and down, our path being parallel with the Alexandria and Manassas wagon road, and just to the north of it. I found I had underrated the distance from our camp to Alexandria, it being nearly two and one-half miles from our camp. We passed the Convalescent Camp, which was situated on the heights to the west of Alexandria, and to the north of Fort Ellsworth, on the same eminence, and in the immediate vicinity of it. It was used as a rendezvous for convalescent soldiers. In the vicinity of this camp was the Stragglers' Camp and the Recruiting Camp, &c.; making, in the aggregate, an immense collection of tents and occupants.

Passing down the road leading from this camp to the east, we came into Alexandria; the distance was, perhaps, one-half mile; the descent being as steep as the roof of a house. From the heights we had just left, we had a splendid view of the country for miles around. The city of Washington, to the north of us, was in full view, the Capitol looming up in the distance. Fairfax Seminary was two miles to the north-west of us, from the tower of which the rebels observed our movements, and signalled them to the enemy, while making our first advance to and inglorious retreat from Bull Run, in 1861.

The city of Alexandria was a short distance to the east, and perhaps one hundred feet beneath us. We had also a good view of the Potomac from this height. Aquia Creek being the base of Burnside's operations in Virginia, this noble stream was covered with vessels of every size and description, plying to and fro, between Aquia Creek, Alexandria and Washington. I stopped in Alexandria until half-past two, p.m.; went down to the wharves, visited the Slave Pens, once used as a rendezvous where slaves were bought and sold, but at the time of my visit used as a place of confinement for deserters, and others who might be found without passes, by the police. I also visited the Marshall House, where Ellsworth was killed; and started from there for camp.

I arrived in time to attend the funeral of one of our boys who died in the hospital the day before. This was the first death that had occurred in our regiment since we arrived in Washington, and the third since the regiment was organized; the other two being killed, first, the drummer of Company D, from Newport, in a fray at Camp Stevens, the second of Company C, on the cars, between Harrisburg and Baltimore. There were but few of our regiment now in the hospital, and none of them dangerously sick.

Saturday, the 29th, was a pleasant day; the night was still and cold. Sunday morning, the 30th, we found the ground slightly frozen, and ice in the tubs about camp one-half inch thick. The weather continued fine as yet. We had fine mornings here, the air was still, and everything seemed delightful. The smoke from the numerous camp fires, made the atmosphere hazy, reminding one of our Indian summer in New England.

CHAPTER 3

Fredericksburg

December 1st, we had orders to march immediately, and at twelve o'clock our brigade were on the move. We passed through Washington just at nightfall, over the bridge which crosses the east branch of the Potomac, and encamped about two miles beyond the city for the night. In the morning we continued our journey along the Maryland side of the Potomac, and so on, from day to day, until our arrival opposite Aquia Creek, on the 6th inst.

We had fine weather until Friday the 5th, when it commenced raining, and at night turning to snow, made our encamping exceedingly unpleasant. We expected to have reached the Potomac Friday night, but the rain softening the road, made our marching extremely difficult and tedious, and at three o'clock we turned into the woods completely jaded, and commenced to pitch our tents, and make ourselves as comfortable as we could, under the circumstances. I could indeed appreciate the discomforts of our situation. I was fortunate in finding some poles in the woods, already cut, and with the help of the boys, made a shed, and covering it with our tents, with the addition of a lot of dry husks, procured from a barn close by for our beds, managed to pass the night quite comfortably.

It stopped snowing early in the night, and at ten, a.m., the next morning, we were on the march again. It was a delightful morning; the mud had crusted over, bearing us up, as we marched, and the sun shining brightly, gave the evergreens by the roadside, covered with snow as they were, a beautiful appearance. At twelve we were upon the banks of the Potomac, with the rest of our brigade, waiting our turn to be ferried to Aquia Creek. It came at last, and at five, p.m., we were aboard of the boat and on our way. At seven we were alongside the wharf, and at eight were off the boat and in line upon the pier, waiting for orders. It was a bitter, cold night, and much impatience was manifest in both officers and privates, at being obliged to wait in this place so long, before moving to our camping ground.

At half-past nine we finally received orders to march off. Passed up the railroad from Aquia to Fredericksburg about two miles, filed to the left, continued on from the road about one-third of a mile, and after another delay of perhaps half an hour, our colonel selected our camp, and we formed upon it, to pass another unpleasant night. The spot selected was in the woods, upon the side of a hill. The heavy wood had been cut, and most of it taken off, but all of the tops, and some of the largest logs were left, all covered with the snow which fell the night before. Everything being wet, it was some time before we could start our fires. But little sleep could be had that night; the most uncomfortable one that the Twelfth Rhode Island Volunteers had experienced. The place we christened Camp Smoke, a most appropriate name for this place.

The first night and the following day it was impossible for us to escape the smoke from our numerous fires, half of it passing into our eyes, and down our throats. We would pass around our fires, the smoke following our coat-tails as we moved along, and fastened to us soon as we stopped; it was impossible to escape it. We stopped at this place until Tuesday morning, the 9th, when the brigade again took up their line of march. We arrived opposite Fredericksburg Wednesday, the 10th, and encamped for the night alongside the Seventh Rhode Island.

The signal guns, ominous of the coming battle, were first fired at five, a.m., the next morning, and at intervals until sunrise, when a fierce cannonading commenced along the whole line in front of the city. At nine, a.m., we received twenty extra rounds

35

of ammunition, three days' rations, threw our knapsacks and extra luggage into a pile, slung our blankets over our shoulders, and moving to within three-quarters of a mile of the city, formed in line of battle, and rested on our arms, ready for the emergency.

In trying to throw the pontoon bridges over, our forces met with determined resistance, and were obliged to shell the city, in order to dislodge the enemy. Being satisfied of the impossibility of crossing the river this day, late in the afternoon we returned to camp. Early in the evening, the cannonading, which had continued through the day, ceased; and two or three regiments crossing over in boats, after a fierce conflict in the streets of the city, finally succeeded in dislodging the enemy, and the bridges were completed. Early in the morning of the next day, the different brigades commenced crossing the river, and occupying the city, ours among the rest.

The main streets of this city run parallel with the river. We took our position opposite the pontoon bridge, in the rear of the second street. This part of the city suffered severely during the shelling of the place the day before, as the fire from the different batteries was directed in this vicinity, in order to demolish the buildings, which were occupied by the enemy's sharpshooters, who were firing upon our troops, rendering it necessary to dislodge them, to complete the bridge. We were fired upon by the enemy while entering the city, their shells bursting about us, but fortunately doing us no injury. They continued firing through the day, throwing an occasional shell as a regiment approached to cross into the city.

From their batteries, they had a good view of the opposite bank of the river, and could see every regiment, as one by one, they approached the bridge. There were quite a number of casualties during the day, in the city, from the bursting of the enemy's shells. They might have done us infinite damage this day, if they had felt disposed to have directed their fire upon the city. Our position during the forenoon, was directly in range of the enemy's batteries, as they fired upon the troops coming over the bridge.

From the place where I stood in the ranks, I could see two defunct rebels, who were killed the day before, while our batteries shelled the city. I took the liberty to go close, and look at the one nearest me. A shell had struck him in the head, cutting the top of it completely off, leaving nothing above the eyes; killing him of course instantly.

From this place I continued on to another street, to see a group of dead bodies. There were sixteen of them, all belonging to a Massachusetts regiment, and who fell the night before, while engaged in dislodging the enemy. They were laid in a row, and buried close where they fell. I could not help thinking, as I gazed upon the mournful scene, of the loved ones at home, who were waiting, watching, and praying for the safe return of these poor men, who, in the dispensation of a mysterious Providence, they never more could see on earth.

I turned away from the sad spectacle to become acquainted with other features of this cruel war. I had passed along several streets, when the rapid firing of the enemy warned me to return to my regiment. The shells were bursting all about us, and I found the regiment on my return already in line, and soon after we moved and took a position in a less exposed situation, where we remained through the night. I went to a house close by, found some boards, returned to the street, where we were ordered to remain, placed one end of these boards upon the sidewalk, the other end resting in the middle of the street, and finding some straw in the neighbourhood, made my bed upon these, and "*laid me down to sleep.*"

Early in the morning, the different regiments were all astir, preparing for the coming battle. The different companies of our regiment were drawn up in line, our haversacks were filled with three days' rations, which consisted of crackers, pork, sugar and coffee, our canteens with water, and moving some half mile farther down the city, we rested on our arms, in readiness to take the part assigned us. While in this place, we were somewhat sheltered from the enemy's shells, which were thrown at different intervals, several of them dropping and bursting in the river, directly in front of us, causing much dodging and twisting, throughout the different regiments.

There was a space directly in front of our position, upon which there were no buildings, close upon the river. This space was occupied early in the forenoon, by the Irish Brigade, and I saw for the first time, Thomas F. Meagher, the general commanding this brigade, well known as the Irish patriot and fighting general. This brigade were called into action early in the day, and moved to the front at once. This was at about ten, a.m.

The booming of cannon and the sharp cracking of the musketry, soon told us that the "ball had opened," and at twelve o'clock, m. we were called upon. Our line was quickly formed, and we moved on. Filing to the left, we passed up a steep hill on the "double quick," and soon came in sight and within range of the enemy's guns, who immediately brought them to bear upon us. The firing becoming too hot for us, we were brought into line, and ordered to lie close to the ground. Down we went, accordingly, into the mud, and the firing partly ceased. Again we rose, and rushed ahead, the artillery playing upon us more furiously than ever.

Gaining a trench, a short distance ahead, we again came to a halt and formed our line anew. Being partially sheltered from the enemy's fire, we stopped long enough to catch our breath, then throwing off our blankets, passed up the bank, and hurried on. Some twenty rods ahead of this trench, the railroad from Fredericksburg to Richmond passes, making a cut some twenty feet deep. Expecting to find a shelter in this from the enemy's fire, we sprang ahead. Upon gaining the bank, with one spring I ploughed to the bottom. I had hoped to find another breathing spell here, but found myself disappointed in this, as the enemy had a battery in position from which they threw shot and shell the whole-length of this cut, and it was here we first came under the fire of their musketry.

We were ordered to gain the opposite bank as soon as possible. The ascent was very steep, and being out of breath, it required much effort on our part to reach the top. I never in my life strove harder than I did to gain the top of this bank. The distance from this place to the position we were to gain, was perhaps forty rods. And this under a scorching fire of musketry and artillery, at short range. We hurried ahead as fast as possible, knowing this to be no place to make long stops. Our regiment at this time was partially broken up, every man knowing the danger, exerted himself to escape it; and by a "double quick," which at this time had become a run, we were fast gaining the position already occupied by the rest of our brigade, which was partly sheltered from the fire of the enemy.

The report of the cannon, the shriek of the shell, its explosion in our midst, the sharp cracking of the musketry, and the whiz of the Minnie ball, (the different missiles ploughing and cutting up the ground in front of us,) furnished a terrible ordeal, through which the Twelfth were called upon to pass.

Thus we hurried on until we gained the position assigned us. Here a hillock, running parallel with our lines, and slightly elevated above the surface of the plain, intervened between us and the enemy. This afforded us some protection, and here within two hundred yards of the enemy's redoubt, our forces came to a halt, and it was only after our arrival here that we could bring our muskets to bear upon the enemy. Our regiment was brought into this action under many disadvantages. It will be remembered, that up to this time we had been in the service but eight weeks, had journeyed from Rhode Island, had established two different camps in Virginia, and just completed a march of one hundred miles.

Tired and worn out with our long and weary march, and before we had time even to form our camp, or obtain anything to eat, beside "marching rations," (hard crackers and salt pork,) upon which we had subsisted for the two weeks previous, and in all our inexperience as to how we should render our compliments to the foe, we were invited across the Rappahannock, and introduced to the enemy. Upon the first start, on going into action, we ascended a hill where scaling ladders would have been an advantage to us. Then followed a feat of fence jumping, passing barns, brick kilns, &c. Through these gymnastic exercises we were conducted by our colonel, ably seconded by our gallant major. The regiment passed these obstacles in good order, and under a heavy fire reached the first trench, where the line was formed anew.

Here our gallant major unfortunately received a severe wound, was placed on a stretcher, and carried to the rear. This threw the whole command upon our colonel, who without assistance, found it extremely difficult to bring the regiment into action in a manner suited to the notions of some of our military brethren, who felt disposed to criticise us. This class of warriors, with a knowledge of military tactics that would hardly enable them when in four ranks to file right and left without blundering, in their criticism showed little judgment and much injustice, towards a brave and loyal regiment.

We retained our position until nightfall, when, having spent our ammunition, we were drawn off the field. It was nearly dark when we were ordered to fall into line, with strict orders to keep as quiet as possible, so as not to attract the attention of the enemy. We accordingly fell in, and moved quickly off. Upon approaching the railroad, the firing which had ceased commenced anew, and raged furiously. Our troops having charged upon the enemy's works, were endeavouring to carry them at the point of the bayonet, but were overpowered and driven back. As we were in range, this charge brought the enemy's fire directly upon us, as we were passing into the railroad cut. We hastened ahead, threw ourselves down and lay as close as possible, waiting for the storm to pass over. As soon as the firing slackened, we hastened to our feet, and hurrying along the track, soon entered the city and were out of danger, and thus ended a day ever to be remembered in the history of the Twelfth Rhode Island Volunteers.

Having as great a dread of going off the field without a blanket, (having thrown mine away upon going into the fight,) as of the few balls that were following us up, I lingered in the rear and managed to secure one. I found a large pile a short distance from the railroad depot, which our regiment in their hurry to escape passed without securing. They had a perfect right to have taken them, if they had chosen to. They suffered severely afterwards for the want of them, and I think if they should go into a fight again under circumstances that should cause them to throw away their blankets, especially in mid-winter, they will take good care to secure another when they come off the field.

While getting my blanket, the regiment passed out of sight and hearing, and coming off the railroad into the street, the only one I could find whom I knew, was A. W., who had halted to catch his breath, having become nearly exhausted in trying to keep up with the regiment. As we could see or hear nothing of the regiment, I persuaded A. to go with me and get a blanket, he being also without one. We then returned to the city, and after awhile found our regiment, in the same place where we started from in the morning, and in this place we stopped for the night.

In my wanderings the day before the battle, I found an unoccupied house a short distance from where our regiment passed the night, and not relishing the idea of lying on the ground in the street, after our hard day's work, with three others with me, I made for it. We found a room furnished with a bed and sofa, and fastening the doors, we appropriated these luxuries to our own particular use, and slept soundly through the night.

In the morning, I went below to the basement of the house, and found quite a number of our boys busy cooking. There was a large cooking-range in the room, and plenty of wood, and finding a barrel of flour in the house, they were having a feast. I also engaged, and mixing up a batter, I contrived to cook me a good breakfast. The regiment remained through the day of the 14th, upon the street, in quiet, and we occupied the room where we passed the night. There was a piano in the room, a large easy chair, beside other furniture, and we had a good time "housekeeping" in our new tenement.

In the morning, finding plenty of soap and water, I took a good wash, and began to fancy myself at home again. I tried to get S. to wash himself. The answer he made was, that he should not until he knew whether his head belonged to himself or to "Uncle Sam." I was quite amused at the idea. It was plainly evident a little water would not hurt S., as he was looking very much like a contraband. We passed the day (Sunday the 14th) quite comfortably. At night, thinking it best to keep with the regiment, we took quarters in the garret of a house, with the rest of our company. We were ordered to lie upon our arms, keep quiet, and be ready for action at a moment's warning.

Towards morning our pickets had a skirmish with the enemy. We were aroused, but the firing, which was quite rapid for awhile, ceased, and we turned in again. In the morning we arose, and were privileged in having another day of rest. This night, as soon as it became dark, the evacuation of the city commenced. This fact we were all of us ignorant of at the time, and from the disposition of the regiment, supposed we had more fighting to do. At dusk we were formed in line, and as soon as it became dark moved down the city, taking the same street we did on the morning of the battle. We ascended the same steep hill, and proceeded quietly to the front. This made some of us catch our breath, as we thought of what we had already passed through while on the same road.

Just inside our pickets, and under cover of a slight eminence, we laid ourselves down. A detail of men was made from the regiment, for picks and shovels, and upon the arrival of these, the whole front rank were called upon, and proceeding to the top of the eminence, commenced throwing up an entrenchment. This, we afterwards learned, was to deceive the enemy, making them think we intended holding the position. About twelve o'clock the front ranks were called in, and forming in line, we quickly and as noiselessly as possible hurried into the city again. It was evident enough to us as soon as we entered the city that it was being evacuated. When we left, a few hours before, the streets were full of soldiers, regiment after regiment, and battery after battery; now hardly a man was to be seen as we passed through the streets.

The hurried tramp of men and horses in the direction of the

pontoon bridges told us our destination. We hurried along, and at one o'clock the morning of the 16th recrossed the bridge, passed up the hill, and proceeded to our camp, where we left our luggage the morning of the 12th. Our major, whom I had not seen since the fight, suddenly appeared upon our arrival in camp, and taking charge of the regiment, placed them in position, giving off orders in a loud tone of voice, which assured us that though severely wounded, he was fast convalescing.

The next day I saw the major again. I could not discover that he was hurt at all from his appearance; I think he bore up remarkably well. Since then, I noticed at the inspection, and in the presence of the brigadier-general, he limped, and seemed quite lame. I could not help thinking of our able major, who endures his sufferings without a murmur, though severely wounded, and contrasting this self-sacrificing spirit with some I hear of who, though loudly defiant, and anxious to lead their men against the enemy, were known to have run from the field in a "Devil take the hindmost" style, reminding me of a passage in Shakespeare—a piece of advice suited to their case—to wit,—

Just doff that lion's hide,
And draw a calfskin round thy recreant limbs.

CHAPTER 4

Falmouth

After the action of the 13th, our regiment selected a camping-ground a short distance north of the spot we occupied the night before the attack. The spot chosen was in a shallow valley, opening to the south, among the stumps of trees, which had been lately cut by the different regiments encamped in the immediate vicinity. We pitched our shelter tents at first, but knowing the necessity of more adequate protection in case of a storm, as soon as we recovered a little from the fatigues of the past fortnight, we commenced to improve our situation as best we could. Quite a number of the regiment had lost their tents in the fight. The quartermaster managed, some ten days after, to get a few, and distributed them. Still one-fourth of the regiment were without a shelter. This class set to work, and made them a shelter of pine boughs, which, though of little use in case of a storm, (which, by the way, held off wonderfully,) were made very efficient while the dry weather continued.

Here, in camp, you might see some curious styles of architecture, some of the men showing an appreciation of a comfortable home, and a good deal of ingenuity in its construction. Others were content with anything, hardly making any effort at all, seeming to have no anxiety or fear of storms, that might be expected at any time, and if coming upon us at this time, would have caused an infinite amount of suffering among this particular class, who, I am thinking, almost deserved to feel the gripes, to repay them the want of a little anxiety and forethought, in a matter evidently so necessary for the protection of their very valuable lives.

I was fortunate in having a piece of a tent, and in company with some of the boys, who also had them, we together went to work, and measuring off a space large enough for us, dug into the ground eighteen inches perhaps, and cutting logs, placed them against the bank, and continued them up three feet from the bottom of the ground. We also built a fireplace in one end of our house, making our chimney of logs closely fitted together, and plastered with clay, topping it out with a pork-barrel. We placed a ridge-pole lengthwise, at a sufficient height to clear our heads, and passed our tents over this, fastening them to the sides. Some of our party had rubber blankets, which we placed over these, and the rest receiving theirs; soon after, we felt quite secure against wind and weather.

We found our fireplace very useful in keeping our house warm and dry, and as we sat and watched the fire, we could almost imagine ourselves at home again. We cast anchor in this spot Tuesday, December 16th. Friday, the 19th, our regiment was appointed to do picket duty, the right of our line to rest at Falmouth, and the left opposite Fredericksburg, along the banks of the Rappahannock, our headquarters to be at the De Lacey House, opposite Fredericksburg.

The enemy occupied the heights opposite us, a mile back from the river, and threw their pickets out opposite ours, and in some places within speaking distance. At first some fears were entertained, lest the pickets might be tempted or provoked to fire upon one another. Instead of this, neither party seem inclined to communicate in this hair-on-end style, but, on the contrary, although strictly forbidden to do so, sometimes held friendly communication with one another. The distance from our camp to the banks of the Rappahannock, was perhaps two miles.

We went on picket regularly, every Friday morning, and remained on twenty-four hours, then returned to camp again. This duty was not very arduous, as our regiment guarded a line of not more than a mile in length, along the river, and held heavy reserves, to repel any force that might attempt to cross from the opposite side. In the daytime, no danger being apprehended from this source, some of the men procured passes, and were allowed to go to Falmouth, where, if they were so fortunate as to have the means, and felt so disposed, could, by paying exorbitant prices, get the wherewith to refresh the inner man.

There is a large mill in this place, which is capable of turning out large quantities of flour and meal. There are twelve sets of stone in the building, six for grinding wheat, and six for corn. I visited this mill, and for the first time, witnessed the operation of grinding, bolting, and packing flour. There were only two sets of stone running for wheat, at the time I visited the mill. There were also two sets grinding corn. Having seen no Indian meal for some time, I bought half a peck, paying at the rate of two dollars per bushel.

There seemed to be a scarcity of provisions among the people of Falmouth, the boys paying fifty cents for a breakfast of warm Johnny cake and coffee. I went to Falmouth in company with Lieutenant Bucklin, who determined to have a breakfast before leaving, and by hunting awhile found a place, and by teasing, obtained a seat at the table, and for once we ate our fill. We had fried pork steak, hot biscuit, hot coffee and syrup, as much of each as we wished.

In talking with Falmouth men, they tell me that last winter was unusually severe, with large quantities of snow and rain. They told me, also, that this winter had been very mild thus far, but that every sixth or seventh winter was apt to be severe, like that of '61 and '62, but that this winter was a fair type of what they usually are in this part of the country. I told them I was surprised to find the weather continuing so mild, with so little rain. I had noticed one feature of the country that gave me some little uneasiness. This was the deep ravines with which the face of the country is indented, and which I supposed were caused by the heavy winter rains, and expected to see an illustration of this kind of drenching and washing, much to my own particular inconvenience. I was told they have their heaviest rains in the summer; this information relieved my mind of that which I had the greatest fear of.

The village of Falmouth is an old, dilapidated looking place, containing, perhaps, one thousand inhabitants. It is situated at the head of tide water, on the Rappahannock, three-fourths of a mile above Fredericksburg, and is connected with the opposite side of the river by a bridge, which crosses directly opposite the centre of the village; half of the bridge, on the Falmouth side, remains uninjured, the rest of the way nothing but the piers remain standing. The length of this bridge was about forty rods, and crossed the river at a height of perhaps thirty feet. It was a wooden structure, and rested on piers of logs and stone. There is a considerable fall in the river, opposite and above Falmouth, the bed of which, at this place, is one mass of rough, broken rocks, extending up the river as far as I could see.

Owing to the long continuance of dry weather, the river is very low, and could be easily forded, I should think, anywhere in the vicinity of this place. I believe it is generally acknowledged to have been a great mistake, in not crossing the river and occupying the heights, now in the possession of the enemy, which could have been easily done at the time our first detachment arrived here. I think one with a good pair of boots could go over dry shod. The bridges were burned at the time of Burnside's occupation last summer. Since then the people about here habitually crossed and recrossed the river with their teams. Our Generals, having had experience last winter, which was unusually rough and stormy, had fears, no doubt, of having their communication cut off if they crossed, through the rise of the river alone, and thus find themselves in a tight place before the railroad bridge could be completed.

The banks of the Rappahannock, at Falmouth and beyond Fredericksburg as far as I could see upon the northern side, are very high and precipitous,—I should think, upon an average, sixty feet above the level of the river. On the Fredericksburg side the bank is not as steep. The heights back of the city, and occupied by the enemy as their first line of defence, and three-fourths of a mile from the river, are but very little higher than those occupied by our batteries immediately upon the bank. Fredericksburg, as we stand on the bank opposite, seems almost beneath our feet, and, of course, at the tender mercies of our batteries. There is a wagon-road between Falmouth and Fredericksburg, upon the northern side of the river, running close by the edge at the foot of the bank. Along this road our line of pickets are stationed. Upon the opposite side, along the river, is the wagon-road occupied by the pickets of the enemy.

Our repulse at Fredericksburg somewhat discouraged the soldiers, but as time passed by they gained courage again. Immediately after the battle, newspapers in opposition to the administration appeared in camp and were sold in large quantities. These scurrilous sheets were eagerly sought after and read by the soldiers of our regiment, who fed upon them like crows upon *carrion*, not considering the object of this abuse of the administration,—namely, *political chicanery*. Some of the men who had enlisted for nine months, no doubt hoped to escape without getting into a fight; but, having seen the *elephant*, and partly caught a glimpse of his gigantic proportions, they were ready to make a sacrifice of every principle of right and justice rather than to expose their *precious lives* again.

Many of these men were those who, at home, were ready to make every sacrifice, denouncing the rebels in no unmeasured terms, shouldering the musket with an alacrity worthy of the cause to which they pledged their "lives and *sacred honour;*" who, after a little experimenting in shot, shell, and gunpowder, were ready to make any sacrifice, or compromise with the enemy, that would relieve them, fully illustrating the old saying that "distance lends enchantment to the view;" also, that "self-preservation is the first law of nature." I became utterly disgusted with this class of croakers and grumblers, whom it was impossible to escape, and who greedily fed upon everything discouraging, namely, "the impossibility of conquering the enemy," "ruinous state of the finances," "depreciation of paper currency," &c., endeavouring to hold an argument upon matters they evidently knew nothing about.

They at this time flattered themselves that a general feeling of dissatisfaction among the soldiers would go towards putting an end to the war, and used their influence accordingly, swallowing and disgorging all things of a discouraging nature, and that with an avidity which would do credit to a flock of buzzards feeding upon a defunct mule. Those were trying times; but the same principle which prompted me to enter the service still upheld me. I had faith to think that, as the war progressed, partisan feeling would be destroyed, the North would become more united in purpose, able leaders would be found, and this rebellion would eventually be crushed.

I was very fortunate in being permitted to enjoy good health thus far. I had not as yet been reported sick, or been excused from duty on account of sickness, and by a little care escaped the tender mercies of our hospital. Sickness at this time, January 19th, began to tell upon the regiment. Quite a number had died in the hospital within a week. Stephen Clissold was the first man of our company who had died in the hospital up to this time. He received a severe wound in the head while in action, December 13th, which I think was the ultimate cause of his death. I am afraid much sickness in this regiment was brought about through the neglect of men, in not being mindful of a few simple things, which go far towards preserving their health.

I know some of the men suffered for the want of clothes, through their own carelessness. This particular class, not considering the irregularity of supplies, especially in connection with so large an army as we had in our immediate vicinity, and the impossibility of keeping a supply constantly on hand, of all kinds, and the necessity of economizing, and keeping in good condition what they had, until they could get more, found themselves uncomfortably short.

Immediately after the battle of the 13th, for two or three days, we were somewhat short of provisions, but had enough to satisfy our hunger. As we became established in camp, we began to live again. At first we had hard crackers. This is the staple article. Then pork, coffee, sugar and beans. After being here two weeks, we drew rations of fresh beef, drawing it regularly since, once a week. We had potatoes two or three times, and onions, also.

January 14th, we drew rations of salt beef; this was the first we had seen since we left "Camp Casey."

January 15th, we drew rations of dried apples, but hard crackers, salt pork and coffee, are the staple articles. These we had at all times, as much as we wished; when on the march it is all we have. Beans and rice we usually had at all times, as they are more easily transported. Beef, potatoes, onions, &c., we began to class among the luxuries of a soldier's life, it being impossible to supply us with these, at all times, during an active campaign. Sutlers, who had not been seen for some time, began to come among us again. I will give the prices of some of their articles, as they were sold at that time: Tobacco, $2 per lb.; butter, 75 cents per lb.; cheese, 50 cents per lb.; pepper, $1 per lb.; apples, 5 cents apiece; cookies, 25 cents a dozen; boots, $8 and $10 per pair, that retail at home for $3 and $4, and other things in proportion. Soft bread was among the things gone by; we had not seen any since we left "Camp Casey."

January 17th, we received marching orders. Packed our knapsacks accordingly, filled our haversacks with rations, and prepared to march at an hour's notice. All things seemed to indicate a speedy move. Sunday, the 18th, passed by. Monday, the 19th, regiment after regiment passed our camp. Tuesday, the 20th, it was evident the "Grand Army" of the Potomac were in motion. This day, at "dress parade," an address from General Burnside was read to us, calling upon us once more to face the enemy. Our colonel had orders to move the regiment that night, or the following morning. At nightfall, the wind, which had been blowing from the south-east for two days, threatening rain, suddenly veered to the north-east, and culminated finally in a storm; consequently we remained in camp. It continued raining until the morning of January 23rd, when it finally ceased.

CHAPTER 5

Camp Life

Since the storm of January 20th, 21st, and 22nd, which will be remembered as defeating the plans of Gen. Burnside in his attempt to cross the Rappahannock, we had much stormy weather, pleasant days being rare curiosities. And although having been wonderfully favoured with pleasant weather up to that time, it became certain we were to have the reverse of it, thereby making the old adage good, that "one extreme begets another."

It got to be a saying among us, that when the 12th Rhode Island Volunteers move, the storm ceases. The 23rd was the appointed day for our regiment to go on picket. In the morning it rained, and showed no signs of clearing off, but immediately upon our regiment's moving the clouds began to disperse, and when we reached Falmouth, the sun came out; and at two, p.m., not a cloud was to be seen. We took up our quarters in an old meeting-house, on the heights of Falmouth, a situation overlooking the entire village, the city of Fredericksburg, and the river, for one mile in either direction.

The village of Falmouth abounded at this time in sutlers, who still held their goods at exorbitant prices. The troops commenced their retrograde movement the morning of the 23rd, and the road was thronged with batteries, baggage wagons, ambulances, and soldiers, moving to their old quarters. Just at nightfall I was in the village, and at that late hour, battery upon battery, ambulance upon ambulance, lined the street, hurrying back to their respective quarters. One need but to have seen this immense amount of war material on exhibition, as we were permitted to, to have been assured of the great strength and effectiveness of the Army of the Potomac, if properly directed. As the enemy were opposed to us at this place in large force, and disposed no doubt for desperate efforts, we expected soon a bloody struggle.

It was deferred by the interposition of a merciful Providence, through the agency of the "God of storms," until a more favourable time. Still I had faith to think that the enemy at this place would be obliged to yield to the immense force we were able to bring against him, and patiently waited the time that would bring shame and defeat to the enemy, and crown our arms with victory. Then can we in the fullness of our hearts and in all truthfulness say, that

> *The star spangled banner in triumph does wave,*
> *O'er the land of the free and the home of the brave.*

In the knowledge of the immense amount of power brought into action by both parties, in this sanguinary struggle, when the science and genius of nearly the whole world are turning their thoughts in this direction, forsaking other and more useful pursuits, some thoughts naturally suggest themselves.

I could not help thinking, that from time immemorial the differences of men upon approaching a certain point, when "forbearance ceases to be a virtue," have always culminated in this summary way of cutting, slashing, and braining one another. Still it seems very unfortunate that these things cannot be settled by other means. History makes no mention of other ways provided, so I trust we are following the appointed way, by laying on "tooth and nail."

From Saturday, 24th, to Tuesday, 27th, the weather was quite warm, with occasional showers of rain. Wednesday morning we found it snowing, the air extremely cold, the wind from the north-east, blowing a gale, which continued through the day, making it the most uncomfortable day we have yet experienced. Thursday, 29th, was sunny, warm and pleasant, and we had no more rain until Sunday, February 1st, when we had to submit to another rainy day, which though unpleasant to us, was the means of clearing off what little snow remained upon the ground. The day before, we were visited by the U. S. Paymaster, and received our pay from the date of enlistment, up to October 31st. Some of the boys were hoping to get their pay up to the 1st of January, but getting it from the date of enlisting, which was more than they expected, (as they thought of obtaining pay only from the time of mustering in, October 13th,) they rested satisfied and waited, if coming short, for the next pay day.

Monday, February 2nd, I had a visit from Joseph S. Davis, of the Twenty-Ninth Massachusetts, whom I had not seen before for years, the same contented good-natured fellow, full of his jokes as ever. Found him minus two fingers, and since then, I hear, by the accidental discharge of his piece, he has mutilated his hand in such a manner as to lay him up for the present. He is now in the hospital at Washington.

Tuesday, the 3rd, was severely cold, the wind blowing strong from the north-east, with frequent snow squalls.

Thursday, 5th, rumours were afloat that we were soon to be removed from our present situation.

Sunday, the 8th, had orders to prepare for a march, with three days' rations, to proceed to Aquia Creek, and from thence by transports to Fortress Monroe. Monday opened upon us pleasantly. This day, at three, p.m., we struck our tents, and bade farewell to "*Camp Mud.*" At half-past four, p.m., we stacked arms, and rested close by the depot, in company with other regiments, awaiting their turn to go aboard the cars. At half-past five, p.m., we hurried aboard, and after the usual delays, we finally started. We proceeded most of the way slowly, and did not arrive at Aquia Creek until ten o'clock in the evening. As soon as we arrived at this place we unloaded from the cars, the regiment was formed upon the wharf, and went immediately aboard the steamers *Metacomet* and *Juniata*, that were waiting to receive us. As soon as the regiment were aboard, they hauled into the stream, where we passed the night.

The morning of the 10th dawned upon us, promising a pleasant day. The long-looked-for schooner *Elizabeth and Helen* from Providence, we learned had arrived during the night, and was laying in the offing. I had just had her pointed out to me, and was looking at her, imagining what might be aboard for me, and wishing for half a bushel of apples to grind on our trip, when I saw a boat put off, and could just discover the head of our colonel above the bow of the boat, making for us. He brought a few boxes for himself and staff, and two barrels of apples for the regiment. The apples were distributed among the men, and were very acceptable; I got two small ones for my share. At half-past eleven, our quartermaster's stores came alongside, were taken aboard, and, weighing anchor, we started down the river. It was a most beautiful morning, and all were in good spirits. I could not help comparing our present mode of transportation with that allowed us while on our march from Alexandria to Fredericksburg, by the way of Maryland and Aquia Creek, two months before.

The Potomac is indeed a beautiful river. Although it is laid down on the maps as being broad and large, still, I had no idea of the magnitude of this noble stream. I should judge that this river, from Aquia Creek to the Chesapeake Bay, was, upon an average, five miles in width. Our steamer, the *Metacomet*, proved a fast sailer. The *Juniata*, which passed us before we started from Aquia Creek, we soon overtook, and as we passed Point Lookout Hospital, at five, p.m., and entered the broad waters of the Chesapeake, the *Juniata* could just be discerned from the stern of the boat. Soon darkness enveloped all, and at nine I turned in. At twelve, by the motion of the boat, I was satisfied that we had reached our destination.

At six, a.m., the 11th, I turned out to ascertain our whereabouts and look upon new scenes. I found the wind blowing fresh from the east, a cloudy sky, and threatening rain. I found we were in Hampton Roads, close in shore, and within three-quarters of a mile of the village of Hampton. There were quite a number of vessels in the Roads—steamers, schooners, gunboats,

&c. Our companion, the *Juniata*, lay a short distance from us, having arrived a few hours later than we.

At about nine, a.m., we started for Newport News. We passed close by the Rip-Raps, a ledge of rocks half way between Fortress Monroe and the opposite shore. Since the war commenced this place has been strongly fortified, and is becoming celebrated as a place of confinement for those incurring military displeasure. We arrived at Newport News, landing at twelve, m., and proceeded immediately to disembark. The appearance of Newport News, I should think, was very much like that of a California seaport. There are two piers built out from the shore, each one perhaps 300 feet in length and 10 feet in width, consisting of spiles driven into the sand, covered with plank, with a railing upon either side to help preserve one's equilibrium.

We filed off the boat upon the pier, passed the length of it, came upon *terra firma*, proceeded up the road, gained the top of the bluff, and filing to the left a short distance, stacked our arms; and, while our colonel went to report himself to his commanding officer, we took the opportunity to become acquainted with the sights and scenes of Newport News.

The *Cumberland*, sunk a year ago by the *Merrimack*, lies opposite the landing, a short distance off in the stream. Her three lower masts and bows are all there is remaining in sight of what was once considered one of the noblest vessels in the service. The hull of the *Congress* lies one mile below, the top of it being plainly visible. It was fortunate the *Monitor* made her appearance as she did, thus putting a stop to the mischief.

This place is of no importance, only as a military post, having been built up since the war commenced. Opposite the landing, the buildings extend from the beach up the bluff, and on to the level space above. The height of this bluff is about 40 feet above high-water mark for a mile or two in either direction from the village, and extending back from this is a level plain, half a mile in width, and in length as far as the eye can reach; and in one continuous line along the bay, upon this level space, the different regiments are encamped, presenting a very fine appearance. The space in front of our camp, one-fourth of a mile in width from the edge of the bluff, is used for drill and parade. The ground from the top of the bluff to the rear descends gradually. Forty rods to the rear of our tents we get plenty of good water.

Our wells are made by digging a hole and inserting two barrels, minus heads, one above the other. There were also ditches, dug parallel with our camp, to the rear of the wells, and being at that time partly filled with water, we had every convenience for washing, and no excuse for dirty faces. In the rear of these ditches at a short distance, are the woods upon which we depended for our fires. Although for the past two years the woodman's axe had told effectively upon these noble forest trees, still there was a good supply left standing. We also depended upon these woods for our music, when all other kinds cease. This being a permanent institution, the denizens of the forest, which included peep frogs and owls, made melody far into the still watches of the night.

The camp of the Twelfth Rhode Island was one-fourth of a mile from the landing, to the north-west. The village of Newport News is enclosed upon the north and west by a palisade and ditch, intended to repel an attack from the rear. In this enclosure were the barracks for the men and the usual space allowed for drill and parade. Outside of this enclosure, upon the east, other barracks have been built. Nearly all the buildings are built of logs; some of them, built for traders and quartermasters' use, are of rough boards, evidently not intended for anything permanent. In extent, these buildings are scattered over an area of half a mile in width and one mile in length along the shore of the bay.

The bay of itself is a beautiful sheet of water, and opposite us was perhaps four miles in width. As we stood upon the bluff, facing the bay, just below upon the opposite side we could discern the opening leading to Norfolk; to the right, we could see the mouth of the James River; and directly at the entrance could be seen one of our gunboats, keeping watch, ready to apprise us of any danger approaching from that direction. In front of us scattered along, were a few craft, whose general appearance bespoke their calling. The *Galena*, which will be recollected as taking part in the attack upon Fort Darling, last summer, lay in the bay opposite us. Although pierced at that time by twenty-eight balls, she still existed, and, judging from her appearance and reputation, would, when called upon to engage the enemy, be able to give a good account of herself.

The *Minnesota* lay one and one-half miles below us. If the *Monitor* had not come to the rescue, instead of the noble vessel lying now before us, in all her beautiful proportions, she would have presented the same sorry figure as the *Cumberland* and *Congress*, undoubtedly sharing the same fate.

Included in the fleet were three gunboats, of the *Monitor* pattern. These boats need no praise, and are particularly expected to speak for themselves.

February 12, the next day after our arrival here, being warm and pleasant, we went into the woods to cut and split logs for our house. The 13th and 14th was occupied in this business. The 15th, those in the tent with me gave out; this brought things to a stand before our house was completed. The 16th it commenced storming; this, of course, put a stop to operations. This day I received a box of apples from home. The 17th, received one-half barrel from Jason Newell. These came in good time.

The storm continued until Friday, the 20th. Saturday, 21st, our colonel ordered all log-huts to be levelled and taken off the ground. This was done. New "A" tents were issued and put up at once. The next day we were to have *straw hats*. (This, I will allow, was mere conjecture on my part.) However, we had just time to pitch our tents before it commenced raining. In the night it snowed; and the following morning we found it raining again, which continued through the day, making it very disagreeable. Upon the whole, the regiment were the better off for the new tents, as many of the boys would make no effort towards building them a house, and having nothing but the "shelter tents," were poorly provided for. But for those who were used to better quarters, the change was submitted to with an ill grace.

Wednesday, the 25th, the 9th Army Corps passed in review before Gen. Dix.

Saturday, March 14, we had a sword presentation, Company F presenting Capt. Hubbard with a beautiful sword, pistol, sword-belt, &c. The money was raised in the company, by subscription, and the articles were purchased and brought on by J. L. Clark, our quartermaster. F. M. Ballou, who had lately received a second lieutenant's commission, and was assigned to Company F, was also presented at the same time with a sword, pistol, sword-belt, cap, and other things, from friends at home. These were also brought on by J. L. Clark, who had just returned to the regiment, after an absence of two weeks.

The camp of the Twelfth Rhode Island Volunteers, at this place, was the finest looking camp on the ground. The streets were well laid out, and were kept swept clean. The tents were new, and presented a neat, uniform appearance.

There was a great improvement in the regiment after coming here. We were well clothed, and as finely equipped as any regiment in the field. We also had the Springfield rifled musket, which is considered the best in the service.

While at this place we had a fray in camp, which came near being a serious affair. I was in the quartermaster's tent the evening of the 5th of March, when at eight o'clock our orderly came in, telling us our company had received a visit from the 48th Pennsylvania, a regiment adjoining, who came provided with clubs and stones, to settle some difficulty which had occurred between them and some of our boys. We had some rough fellows in our company, and upon the Pennsylvania boys making their appearance, at it they went. After a few rounds the intruders retreated. No one of our company was dangerously wounded; a few slight cuts about the head and ears included the whole list of casualties.

Soon after this affair I returned to my quarters and turned in, hoping to have a good night's rest. In about half an hour we were apprised of another visit from our neighbours. Out our boys rushed, crying *Turn out! turn out! drive 'em! drive 'em!* At the same time, we could hear the clubs strike against the sides of our tents. Immediately after I heard Captain Hubbard rush along, and soon after the report of a pistol, one, two, three, followed by the report of a rifle, assured me that it was time to pull on boots and prepare for battle. Upon coming from my tent I found the tumult had subsided. Our lieutenant-colonel came along, we were all ordered to our quarters, and the guard being called upon, this fray, which promised something serious, was finally quelled. I did not hear that any one was seriously hurt.

The next morning, as I lay in my tent, looking out upon the street, a party of three or four stopped in front for a talk. Soon one of them began to show symptoms of a strange nature, and directly over he went upon his back. In connection with the affair of the past night, I began to think things were coming to a crisis. However, the man, who to all appearance was dead, by dint of hard rubbing, applied by those gathered around him, was at length brought to and carried off.

Chapter 6

Kentucky

March 18th a cold, disagreeable storm commenced, lasting till the 21st; it commenced with a drizzling rain, which finally, however, turned into a stiff snow storm, and on the morning of the 21st it cleared off, the snow lying on the ground six inches deep. All were now looking forward to the time when we should pull up and leave for other parts.

March 23rd, the snow had disappeared, much to our satisfaction. This day was spent in issuing clothing to the regiment. They were now fully prepared for the journey before them. The Twelfth at this time was the largest regiment in the entire corps, and the finest in its general appearance, as regards the men, their clothing, arms, equipments, &c.

Wednesday, 25th, we received marching orders.

Thursday, 26th, at seven, p.m., we struck our tents and remained in the streets, waiting for orders to fall in. Meanwhile, fires were kindled, and a general bonfire ensued; sticks, poles, boxes, and everything that would burn was scraped up and added to the flames. It being a cold, chilly night, these fires proved very cheering and comfortable. At eleven in the evening we were called upon to fall in. This was quickly done; the regiment was formed, and we immediately proceeded to the landing, and went aboard the steamer *Long Island*, and were soon on our way, bidding farewell to Newport News, where we had spent many pleasant hours, much to our own comfort individually, and with profit to the regiment. The morning of the 26th we were steaming up the Chesapeake, *en route* for Baltimore.

Left the Chesapeake at six, p.m., entered the Petapsco, and at seven were brought alongside the wharf, where we passed the night.

At six o'clock on the morning of the 27th we were ordered to sling knapsacks. This done we filed off the boat, the regiment was formed, and marching through the streets of the city, we stacked our arms opposite the depot, and were to go aboard the cars as soon as the necessary arrangements could be made. The boys were allowed to leave the ranks and go where they chose. I went down street, and found there was plenty of liquor to be had, and also that it was in *great demand*; many of the boys were getting their canteens filled, &c.

The people of Baltimore were very friendly to us. As we marched through the streets we met with cordial greetings; handkerchiefs were waved, flags were displayed, &c. This was reciprocated by the regiment, who answered back in deafening cheers.

We had our hands full after starting from Baltimore, in consequence of the boys indulging too freely in "whiskey libations." They had seen no liquor for some time, and seemed determined to make the most of this. At twelve we commenced entering the cars, and at one p.m. the regiment were all aboard. Some of the men were picked up and brought on in a dilapidated condition, having been engaged in turning *somersaults*, evidently having had help in this game, judging from the countenances of some of them, which had materially changed, showing marks where the fist had been too closely applied for the good of the recipient, resulting in *crawls upon all four*, and other demonstrations of a like character.

With three or four exceptions, all of our company came aboard without help, though I am sorry to say many of them were full of fight, and commenced operations soon after entering the cars. It fell upon me to stand at one end of the car, with orders to allow no one to go out, under any pretence, as in the present condition of the men the result no doubt would have been disastrous. Soon the uproar commenced, which continued until darkness put a stop to it. There would be an occasional lull in the tempest, as parties became exhausted.

Towards night, those who were brought aboard insensible, and who were indebted to a few of us for their preservation—as the chances were that they would have been stamped to pieces if we had not exerted ourselves to save them—came to and *sailed* in for their share. Such an uproar I never heard among human beings, and it required our utmost exertions to keep them from annihilating one another. Darkness came upon us at last, the uproar partly ceased, and comparative quiet reigned in this *menagerie*.

The train was started at two, p.m., and proceeded slowly throughout the afternoon. Late in the evening we stopped at Little York, Penn., where hot coffee and bread were served to such of the regiment as felt disposed to partake. We were now fairly on our way, *en route* for the West, *via* Harrisburg. After leaving Little York we proceeded rapidly, and the next morning, at eight o'clock, stopped at Lewistown, Penn., sixty miles to the west of Harrisburg.

March 28th, at half-past one, p.m., stopped at Altoona, where hot coffee and white bread were served to us. At quarter-past two commenced the ascent of the Alleghany Mountains. Our train consisted of thirty cars, drawn by a powerful locomotive. Upon commencing the ascent of the mountain, two more were attached, one to the rear of the train, and one ahead. The road is very crooked, and the train, as it moved slowly, winding its way along the numerous curves, like some huge serpent, presented to the eye of the beholder a novel and beautiful spectacle. In many places we could look down into ravines several hundred feet in depth, close beside the track, the sides of which were nearly perpendicular; and upon the other hand the mountains would rise as high above us.

All along the road the mountains were covered with a heavy growth of timber. Millions of logs, of all sizes, lay rotting upon the ground, seeming ready to tumble upon us at any moment.

This crossing the Alleghanies presented features of a kind new to Rhode Islanders, and was enjoyed by all who could appreciate the beauties of nature.

At half-past two, p.m., we passed through the tunnel at the summit and commenced our descent. Passed Johnstown at six, and at twelve entered Pittsburg. At half-past twelve, the morning of the 29th, the regiment left the cars and marched to the City Hall, the general rendezvous for supperless soldiers. We here found supper awaiting us, to which we quickly introduced ourselves. Had white bread and butter, crackers, pickles, apples and hot coffee served to us. We were also treated to music from one of the city bands. Stopped an hour in the hall, when the colonel, making a speech, thanking the Pittsburgians for their hospitality, &c., we left, highly pleased with our entertainment. From the hall we marched a short distance and *took lodgings* under the shelter of a large shed adjoining the depot, where some of us were so fortunate as to get a short nap.

At six, a.m., rose from my downy bed, visited a saloon close by, had a good wash, and through the kindness of a friend, a good breakfast of potatoes, hot biscuit, beefsteak, coffee, &c. At half-past nine, a.m., the regiment entered the cars, and at ten the train started, crossing the Alleghany River, *en route* for Cincinnati, via Steubenville and Columbus. I improved the little time I was in Pittsburg in looking about me. I was somewhat surprised at the general appearance of the city. I had often heard it spoken of as a dirty place. We often hear it called the city of "Eternal Smoke." This proceeds from the numerous forges, furnaces, and so on, which abound in the city, its principal business being the working of iron, for which it is celebrated.

In connection with its business I had pictured in imagination a collection of low, heavy buildings and dilapidated houses, all of the colour of smoke. Instead of this, I found a place of great beauty and interest. Many of the buildings in the business portion of the city were four and five stories high, brick and stone being the material used. All of the buildings were neat in appearance, and many of them models of taste and beauty in their architecture. I saw very fine looking churches in this place. Owing to our short stay here, I cannot enter into a description, but judging from what I saw, should think it a place of great wealth, uncommon beauty and interest. We passed through Steubenville, Ohio, at two, p.m.

At the village of Means, a short distance beyond, halted for coffee. Halted again at the village of Newcomerstown, at seven, p.m., at the village of Cheshocton, at nine, and at the city of Newark at twelve. All along through these villages we were warmly welcomed by the inhabitants. The ladies ran to meet us as we came to a halt. Many of them brought bread, pies and apples to the soldiers. Some of the boys were the recipients of little tokens of affection, in the shape of kisses. Relative to the kisses, "Freely as you receive, freely give," was the rule on the part of the boys. While passing through these villages, for my share, I received an apple and a slice of white bread and sauce.

Monday, 30th, at two in the morning, the train came to a halt again, and upon making inquiry, I learned we had arrived at Columbus, the capital of the State. Here we found refreshments for the whole regiment awaiting us. White bread was brought into the cars and given to those who wished it. Before the coffee could be brought to us, our colonel, thinking the regiment needed rest more than coffee and bread, (many of them being asleep at the time,) ordered the train to pass on. Not having a good chance to sleep myself, I being ready to eat and drink all I could get, I secured four loaves of the bread, and finding the coffee was in the depot, I hastened from the cars and was in time to fill my canteen.

At seven, a.m., we passed through Zenia, where the train stopped long enough for us to wash up and look about us. Starting from here, at ten, a.m., we made a halt in Miami Valley, at a little village, where we remained until noon. At the village of Morrow we stopped four hours. This delay was owing to a train ahead of us smashing up, obliging us to wait till the track could be cleared. At five, p.m., we started again, and at seven entered the city of Cincinnati. After a delay of an hour we alighted from the cars and soon after proceeded to the Fifth Street Market, where supper was provided us. Our refreshments were the same as those we had at Pittsburg minus the music.

At nine, p.m., we retired from the hall, after acknowledging our thanks by three deafening cheers, and marched immediately to the boat, which we found awaiting us, and at ten, p.m., were across the Ohio and standing on Kentucky soil. We landed in Covington, a place opposite Cincinnati. At eleven, we turned in for the night, occupying the floor of an old, dilapidated shed, near the depot.

Tuesday, 31st, our colonel endeavoured to get us a breakfast for the regiment at this place, but was unsuccessful. Our haversacks furnished us a breakfast at this place. We were delayed here until one, p.m., when we again took the cars and were soon hurrying on, *en route* for Lexington. Passed through the town of Belmont at four, and arrived at Lexington at nine in the evening. Here we had arrived, we learned, at the end of our journey. We took up our quarters for the night in the cars and about the depot.

Wednesday, April 1st, turned out at an early hour, kindled fires, made coffee and took our breakfast. The regiment was not called upon to fall in until half-past eight, a.m. Meanwhile I took the opportunity to visit the grave and monument of Henry Clay, which are in the cemetery a short distance from the depot. The monument is very large, and upon the top of the tall shaft stands a statue of the departed statesman. His grave is about forty rods from the monument. It was pointed out to me by one familiar with the spot. It is ten feet north of the monument erected by him to the memory of his mother, Mrs. Elizabeth Clay, formerly Watkins. There are no stones to mark the spot where he lies, as his remains will undoubtedly soon be removed to the vault prepared for them, at the base of the monument.

Finding some coffee beans, as they call them here, upon the grave, and which grew upon a tree overshading it, I secured them for a memento. I also visited the place allowed for the burial of soldiers who die in the hospitals here. The space allotted is upon an eminence, and the manner of burying is novel and interesting.

The graves were arranged in circles, the first circle enclosing a space twenty feet in diameter, with the foot of the grave towards the space, and the head outwards. The second circle outside of this, and so on. There were several circles already finished. The space is reserved for the erection of a monument at some future time. There are many fine specimens of sculpture in this cemetery, and monuments in great profusion. At half-past eight we were called upon to fall in, and immediately marched to our encampment. This was situated upon the Fair Grounds, three-quarters of a mile from the city. It was a beautiful situation, amid a grove of black walnuts and maples, commanding a fine view of the surrounding country, which includes many interesting localities. The Ashland Estate, well known as the residence of Henry Clay, is but a mile from our camp. This estate is very large, comprising originally one thousand acres.

Thursday, April 2nd, I started on a visit to this place. Just before reaching the house we came upon two children, a boy and a girl, who were playing in a grove adjoining. They were about ten or twelve years of age. Upon coming up to them to make some inquiry, I noticed in the features of each a striking resemblance of the man whose memory we hold in reverence. Upon making inquiry, I learned they were grand children of Henry Clay. Their father, James Clay, was absent, holding a high position in the rebel army; his family occupying the homestead. It was a very warm, pleasant day, and the whole family, which consisted of the mother and two other younger children, were busying themselves outdoors, and looking at the men who were employed at the time of our visit, in the garden.

The wife of James Clay is a woman apparently about thirty years of age, in height rather below the average; has black eyes and hair, is of a dark complexion, and without doubt in her younger days was considered handsome. Her countenance bears the traces of grief, and in the absence of her husband, she is no doubt seeing trouble. I had a talk with one of the men respecting the family. He showed me the house he lived in, which is situated on the estate, and was rented to him by Mrs. Clay the year before. He said he was a Union man, and thought it best she should understand it so, before he occupied the premises. He therefore told her. All she told him was that she rented the house for the money. Whether her husband's course is approved of by her or not, he could not ascertain, as she keeps her own counsels. I was told the whole family since the death of the honoured parent, which occurred some eight years ago, have dressed in black. Mrs. Clay was dressed in a full suit of deep mourning. In connection with her husband's position at the present time, I thought the dress very appropriate.

We were allowed the privilege of going about the premises. I learned that the house occupied by the elder Clay had, since his decease, been removed, giving place to one more modern in its style of architecture. There has been no alteration made in the outbuildings, of which there are quite a number. The house is a very fine building, built of brick, with free-stone cornices, window caps, &c. The lawn is very spacious; around the outer edge is a carriage road, and upon either side of this is a row of trees. The principal kinds are hemlock, firs and black walnuts, most of them of large size. Scattered about the lawn in great profusion are others of different kinds. Alongside the carriage road were a few neglected flower beds. Finding some of them in bloom, I culled one and sent it home as a memento of my visit to this celebrated estate.

After a short stay here, we returned to camp. On our way back we passed the residence of John Clay, and took the opportunity of visiting his stables, and seeing the horses owned by him, he being reputed the owner of some of the finest horses in the State. We found the stables easy of access, several negroes being in charge, who were willing to show us about the premises. This Clay is quite a sporting character; has a race course of his own, and makes a business of rearing and racing horses. Those we saw were the finest he had. One of them, a bright bay mare, named Edgar, is said to have run her mile in one minute forty-six seconds. Those I saw were all trained to running.

On our way from the stables we passed the house. Being hungry, I inquired of a negro if he could find us something to eat. He took us up to the house and asked the inmates of the kitchen, which consisted of three negroes, one man and two women, if they could do anything for us. The man said that Mr. Clay was sick, and had refused several before us. Finding we would accept of a johnny-cake which was cooking upon the stove, he took it off and gave it to us. The widow of Henry Clay resides at this place with her son. She is now in her eighty-third year, is very feeble, and will soon follow her lamented husband to the tomb.

From here, returning to camp, we stopped to see a herd of mules that had just been turned loose, and who were capering and cutting around at a break-neck rate. Occasionally one would stop and let fly a pair of heels, making all crack again. I could not see as there was any damage done, however. Oftentimes two or three, while upon the full run, would go down upon the ground, and coming up again, run as fast in another direction. Such thumps as they gave one another would kill anything but a mule. At one, p.m., I reached camp, much pleased with my journey.

Sunday, April 5th, I attended church in the city, in company with two or three hundred of the regiment. Monday, 6th, signed pay-roll, and the next day, the 7th, were paid off, receiving our pay up to the 1st of March. We had been in camp here a week, and were getting pretty well established. Our quartermaster, J. L. Clark, was left at Newport News to settle up affairs there, and then was to follow us with the major part of the luggage. At this time, April 7th, he had not reached us. Through some one's fault, we were on short allowance while at this place, and as we begun to live again, received marching orders.

Wednesday, the 8th, broke camp, and started on our march at eight, a.m., accompanied by the rest of the brigade. It was a warm, pleasant morning. We passed through the city, and took the road in the direction of Winchester, and after a very severe march of twenty-two miles, we reached our encampment, which was situated two miles south of this village, at half-past seven in the evening. This was a hard day's march for the first brigade. The road over which we passed, ran in a south-easterly direction from Lexington, in a straight line.

Underneath the surface of the ground are ledges, which abound in this part of the country, of slate and sandstone. These are easily worked, and are the material used in making roads. The stone is broken in small pieces, which in course of time become fine, making an excellent thoroughfare. The road throughout its whole length was made after this manner. Owing to the material used in making and repairing, (every little way having to walk over stones lately carried on,) it was very hard for the feet. I have not been able to learn that there was any necessity of our making this two days' march in one, except perhaps to gratify the caprice of Col. Griffin of the Ninth New Hampshire, who commanded the brigade in the absence of Gen. Naglee. But a small portion of the brigade managed to reach camp the night of the 8th. Many of the men carried heavy knapsacks, and were obliged to fall out. After marching a few miles, I judged from the motion of things that they were intending to make the march in one day. I therefore fell out, took off my boots, and put on a pair of "whangs," so as to march as easy as possible.

Just before taking my place in the ranks again, I came across my chum, who had dropped out to rest, his feet already blistered. As it would be easier to march in the rear of the regiment, thereby avoiding the dust, (it being a very dusty road withal,) and rest at his leisure, he had made up his mind to do so. Our things being together, I kept him company. After marching some sixteen miles this way, my companion, who was about used up, halted until the baggage wagons came up with us, and contrived to get his knapsack into one of them, and soon after found a place for mine. This made it easier for us. The wagons belonged to the brigade, and I was fortunate in getting my knapsack on one containing baggage of the Twelfth Regiment.

My companion, after our arrival in the village, took his off and slung it on his back again. Finding the wagon containing mine was to accompany our regiment, I concluded to let it remain there. As soon as the wagon started, I seized hold of it, and by that means contrived to keep up, the team some of the way going upon the trot. We finally reached camp. I was about five minutes getting my knapsack off the wagon, my blankets out of it, and in turning in. My chum turned in for the night under a fence, about quarter of a mile in the rear, being pretty much "played out."

Kentucky is the finest country I have seen yet. It had the same appearance all the way from Lexington to Winchester. The soil to all appearance is excellent, and easily cultivated. The surface of the ground undulates in hill and dale, just enough to give relief and beauty to the scenery. No stones upon the surface to add to the labour of its cultivation. There are no underbrush growing in the woods here. This adds greatly to the beauty of this country, every forest having the appearance of the most beautiful groves, underneath which grass grows in abundance. This gives Kentucky the advantage over any State thus far, that I have seen; and the first in rank, as a cattle producing country, as every forest affords excellent pasturage for the herds of cattle, mules, &c., which abound in this State. The fields are laid out large, are well fenced, and a large part under cultivation. The houses are scattering, being from half a mile to a mile apart, suggesting to a New Englander the idea of others between, in the event of the war coming to an end, together with the institution of slavery. God forbid that this fair land should longer be blighted by this curse.

> *Then conquer we must, when our cause it is just,*
> *Let this be our motto: 'In God is our trust.'*
> *And the star spangled banner, in triumph shall wave,*
> *O'er the land of the free, and the home of the brave.*

CHAPTER 7

Living off the Land

Our brigade comprised the Second Maryland, the Ninth New Hampshire, the Seventh and Twelfth Rhode Island Volunteers, and the Forty-Eighth Pennsylvania regiments, and were under the command of Gen. Naglee. The Forty-Eighth Pennsylvania were assigned to Lexington, to do provost duty, and were left behind. By the way, while at Newport News we had an abundance of all things which it is possible for a soldier to expect. The schooner *Elizabeth & Helen,* of Providence, R. I., which arrived at that place February 16th, laden with vegetables, added to our health and comfort, and the condition of the regiment improved very materially. After leaving Newport News, and up to this time, April 14th, we had nothing but "marching rations," (hard crackers and salt pork,) excepting what was issued at Lexington April 6th, and what we had been able to buy.

The commissary department of the First Brigade was now in working order, and ready to issue rations, April 13th, but our regimental commissary was tardy again, as at Lexington, and our officers slumbered. We had plenty of "hard crackers," but these had become a drug with us, consequently we were tempted to buy what was brought into camp, for which we paid exorbitant prices. The Kentuckians here were aware of our coming, and seemed determined to make the most of us. Some of our officers, whose business it was to attend to these matters, did not consider that the soldier in the ranks might be obliged to study economy, and consequently desire the prompt issue of rations, and some little degree of care and ingenuity in their preparation; thereby saving them the expense of paying out here and there so much for these luxuries.

They did not seem to consider the responsibility resting upon them. Perhaps they did not care. The thing was just here. In each company were from fifty to seventy-five men, whose case was made better or worse, according as their officers were watchful or slumbering. If they had been awake, rations would have been drawn with promptness, and properly cooked; and the consequence would have been that having enough to eat from their own kitchen, the men would have bought the less outside; thereby saving in the aggregate, a large sum which in many instances was needed at home.

Chickens, weighing two and three pounds, were sold here a year ago for one dollar per dozen. This year they sell for two dollars per dozen. Poultry brought into camp in small quantities, sold readily at prices varying from twenty-five cents to one dollar and fifty cents apiece. This included the chicken of two pound and the turkey of eighteen pounds. Small quantities of eggs were brought into camp, and sold at prices varying from fifteen to forty cents per dozen. They were in demand and commanded any price. Pies were brought on in great abundance; they were made of peaches and apples, and sold for twenty-five cents apiece. Some, having a little mercy on the soldier, sold for ten and fifteen cents. Peaches are very plenty in this part of Kentucky, and are preserved and dried in large quantities.

The morning of April 15th finding nothing to eat but hard crackers and pork, and no coffee cooking, I determined to act as commissary for one day at least. I called on A. W., of Company H, and together, at seven, a.m., we left camp, and started off across the fields. We passed the houses nearest camp, and after going about a mile, stopped at a log shanty. This was occupied by a negro family, who were owned by the occupant of a house adjoining. The owner was absent, and the negroes had no authority to sell anything. We were hoping to have found something to eat here, but having nothing on hand cooked, we concluded to go farther.

However, we prevailed on them to cook us some cakes, which we were to call for on our return. Half a mile further on, we came to a large house. The only person we could find here was a negro woman. She could sell us nothing. The next place we called at was owned by one Dr. Evans. Here we found the family at home and busy, preparing to go to camp, with a load of pies, cakes, chicken pies, &c. We intended to have got a breakfast at this place, but the family being very much engaged in their speculation, we continued on.

Espying a house to the right, off some half a mile from this place, we made for it. We were greeted upon our arrival by about half a dozen negro children, who looked upon us with as much curiosity as boys would at home upon the "horned owl" on exhibition. We asked for the woman of the house. She happened to be out of doors at the time, and was pointed out to us. We introduced ourselves, and asked her if she could get us a breakfast. She answered in the affirmative, and asked us into the house. This was a large log-house, and was the one occupied by the owner of the premises. The negroes occupied two or three smaller ones in the same yard, and some five rods distant from the main building.

This is the way the buildings are arranged by the country farmers in this part of the State. The negroes all occupy log-houses. Some of the owners have nothing better, and inhabit the same; but most of them have frame houses, and many of these are large and elegant. The negro women have charge of all the children, both white and black, and the cooking for all is done in the out-houses. We were well entertained at this place. The woman of the house was apparently about seventy-five years of age, and was very intelligent and sociable. Her husband owns a large farm, and some fourteen or fifteen negroes. They raise hemp, keep sheep, spin and weave, as our folks did at home fifty years ago. They have suffered from the raids of the enemy, principally in the loss of horses, not having enough left to cultivate their farms. This is indeed a serious loss to them.

After the lapse of half an hour, our breakfast was brought to us. We had hot biscuit, fried bacon, johnny-cake, butter and milk. We bought five pounds of butter at this place for twenty-five cents a pound, and four dozen of eggs, for which we paid twenty-five cents per dozen. We went beyond here one mile, and procured three dozen eggs more. From here we started on our return to camp. Stopped at a house, and finding the owner absent on an expedition to camp, I prevailed on the negroes to bake us some cake. Here we stopped three-quarters of an hour, during which time the women cooked enough to fill my haversack, for which they charged me twenty-five cents. Leaving here, we called at the place we first stopped at in the morning, and found our bread awaiting us—one large johnny-cake, and one loaf of white bread. This finished our load, and at one, p.m., we arrived in camp, prepared to live again.

We had a most beautiful camp at this place. It was situated in a grove, at a spot where we had every convenience necessary in the shape of wood and water, with plenty of grass to roll and tumble upon. The trees in this grove were perhaps forty feet apart from one another on an average. These consisted of maple, cherry, black walnut, and the common shell-bark, and many of them were of large size. The ground underneath was swept clean, and all brush, chips, &c., removed.

We had "brigade guard mounting" here at nine, a.m. The band would strike up at precisely nine o'clock, and as we watched the movements of the guard as they approached simultaneously from their different regiments to take the place assigned them, we were struck with the beauty of the scene. The guard approaching, take their places, and the music ceases. The "camp guard" upon the right of the line, with nothing but gun and equipments; the "picket" upon the left, with canteen, haversack and blanket, in addition. The line being formed, the sergeant-major, who arranges it, makes a "present" to the officer commanding, and immediately takes his place upon the left.

After he gets his position, the order is given "front." Upon this, the commissioned officers march twelve paces in front of the line, the sergeants eight, and the corporals four. The officer in command advances and gives special instructions to all the officers in person. He then returns to his position, and gives the order, "officers and non-commissioned officers, about face," "inspect your guards." The officers return; the corporals take their places in line; the lieutenants inspect the front rank, the sergeants the rear. The band play during inspection. Inspection over, the music ceases, and the officers take their places in line again. Then comes the order, "music, beat off."

The band commences playing a "slow march," and, coming to the front, proceed the length of the line. After going through the manoeuvres, which bring them to an "about face," they return playing a quickstep, and take their former position. Then the order, "by platoons! right wheel! march!" Immediately upon the completion of the half wheel, which brings them from line of battle into column, the order is given, "pass in review! column forward! guide right! march!" The band strike up, the first platoon make a left half wheel, and march forward, preceded by the band. The other platoons coming up, wheel upon the same spot of the first. After marching forward a certain distance, another left half wheel is made.

Marching straight forward from this, they pass the "officer of the day," who takes the position directly in front of the centre of the line, as it was before moving vacated by the officer in command of the guard, who places himself upon the right of the first platoon, and directs the movement of the column. As each platoon passes in front of the "officer of the day," the officers in charge of their respective platoons come to a "present," saluting, and pass on,—the "camp guard" to the relief of the "old guard," the "picket" to the place assigned them—the band cease playing, and the review ends. The brigade guard mounting, of which I have endeavoured to give a description, is a beautiful and imposing spectacle.

Although the soldier endures many hardships and privations, still there are many pleasant scenes and associations connected with a soldier's life; and I think that should the war continue, many of the men, looking back upon the pleasant side of their campaign, will have a yearning for the scenes and associations in connection with it, and again enter the ranks.

God grant they may! and with willing hearts and hands, and with the assurance of the righteousness of the cause for which they contend, may they consecrate themselves anew to the cause of Freedom.

CHAPTER 8

Boonesboro'

Thursday, 16th. At five, p.m., we received marching orders, with instructions to "pack knapsacks," and be ready to march immediately. At six, p.m., we struck tents, and in half an hour were marching, in company with the rest of the brigade, in the direction of Boonesboro'; and, after a short march of five miles, encamped for the night on the heights which form the banks of the Kentucky River, at nine o'clock in the evening.

Friday, 17th. We did not move from our camp until ten, a.m., owing to the delay necessary in crossing the river. The cavalry accompanying us commenced crossing early in the morning, and at ten, the Twelfth were ordered to fall in. After a march of a mile, we came upon the edge of the river, at the place of crossing, in time to see the last of the cavalry pass over. The river at this place was, perhaps, fifty rods in width, and the convenience for crossing were two scows, in each of which forty men could be taken over at once, and so shaped that our teams could drive on or off at either end. The river was not deep at this place, and the mode of propelling was by pushing with poles.

Some very amusing incidents occurred in connection with our passing over the Kentucky River. Some of the teams, consisting of a government wagon and four mules each, were in readiness, and crossed at the same time with our regiment. This was accomplished by ending the scow on shore, and driving the team on and into the forward part of the boat. The remaining space was filled with soldiers. The scow was pushed across, and, landing end on, the team was driven off. The manner of driving a mule team is this: The driver sits upon the near wheel mule, uses one rein, and by dint of some little hallooing,—understood only by those versed in muleology,—manages his team. The scows were barely wide enough to admit the wheels of the carriages, and it required no little degree of skill to drive on and off without accident. While driving one of the teams off, the near wheel mule, being crowded, jumped off the scow, throwing his rider head and ears under water. The man, upon gaining the surface, was soon ashore; and the mule, after floundering awhile, got a foothold on shore, and the wagon was drawn off. No harm done as we could see to either the mule or his driver.

The next team that crossed, the rider, hoping to profit by the misfortunes of the one in advance, dismounted and attempted to lead his team off. This time, crowding again, over goes one of the mules into the stream, back downwards, hanging in the harness, its head just out of water. This looked like a desperate case of broken legs, and death by drowning. After some little effort, however, the mule was loosed from the harness, the carriage was drawn off by the remaining three, and the unlucky one, through the combined efforts of half a dozen men, was finally drawn from the river, thoroughly drenched, otherwise, to all appearance, not damaged at all.

Ours was the third company across, and passing up the bank, we continued on half a mile, and rested there until the rest of the regiment joined us.

The Kentucky River at this place is bounded upon either side by a range of hills, near akin to mountains. As we approached the river previous to crossing, many novel and interesting scenes presented themselves to our view, reminding us of our journey across the Alleghanies, our first experience in such mountainous regions. From our camp, where we passed the night, upon the heights, the road to the ferry wound along the sides of the hills, and through ravines. In this way the river was gained by gradual and easy descent. As we left camp, the beautiful fields, the green hills, and grassy vales, disappeared; giving place to rough, precipitous hills, whose rocky sides presented quite a contrast to the scenes we left behind.

As we neared the river, directly in front of us, and to the left upon the opposite side, was a ledge of limestone, rising from the surface of the water which washes its base, to a height of three hundred feet, in a nearly perpendicular line, its surface, with the exception of seams and *crevasses*, smooth and white as marble. This was an approximation to the grand and sublime, and to us, inexperienced in such scenes, a beautiful spectacle. The river rolling sluggishly along at this place, deeply imbedded in the hills, could not be seen by us until we were upon its very edge. At the place of crossing the road terminates; and at the opposite side is the terminus of the road, which approaches from the opposite direction. As we came upon the river, upon the same side are two or three houses, with barely arable land enough adjoining to make a garden spot for the occupants. Upon the other side, we found more buildings, and in the immediate vicinity of the ferry considerable land under cultivation.

While here, I learned we were in the immediate vicinity of where Daniel Boone lived. And it was here the first settlement of Kentucky by the whites commenced. I saw the spot where he built his fort, and where he managed to resist the attacks of the Indians, who had determined to eject him from his hermitage. I also filled my canteen from Boone's Spring, so called in honour of the old hero. And as I took a draught from its clear waters, I thought how often he had visited the spot for a similar purpose, and wondered at the courage and perseverance of the man, who could exist in this lonely place, surrounded by hostile Indians; dependent alone upon his own resources, even for his own existence, with no other earthly reliance than his own strong arm, and felt I could do homage to the undaunted bravery and perseverance of the Kentucky pioneer.

We stopped one hour for the rest of the regiment to join us, and then began the slow and toilsome work of ascending the hills. It was a very warm day, and though resting often, the march was a tedious one. Before reaching the top, we halted for the rest of the brigade to come up. This was about two, p.m. Starting again, we soon reached the summit of the hills, and emerged once more into a country beautiful as the one we had left behind us. At the junction of the river road with the Lexington and Richmond pike, we rested two hours.

At this place, Gen. Naglee and staff passed in advance of us, and selected our camp ground for the night. The spot selected was about three miles from this place, and four from Richmond. We reached it at seven, p.m. At six, p.m., while on our way, the Fourteenth Kentucky Cavalry passed us, begrimed with dust, and looking like war-worn veterans, as they really are. Their experience has been with the guerrillas that invest this State, and whom they fight with a vengeance. They had a look of determination, and I have no doubt rebels falling into their hands, find themselves in a tight place.

Saturday, the 18th, at seven in the morning, we started again, passing through Richmond at ten, a.m., and at eleven were resting on our camping ground, two miles beyond. Upon this ground, and in the vicinity, the Battle of Richmond was fought, August 30, 1862, in which the Federals were defeated, losing 150 killed and 350 wounded. Gen. Munson was taken prisoner, and Gen. Nelson was severely wounded in this engagement. The trees about here bore marks of the struggle which ensued. Many of the branches were torn off, and in the trunk of one large cherry tree, I counted seven ball holes. It was a desperate struggle against odds, the enemy outnumbering us four to one. One of the boys, while we were here, brought a shell in, which he picked up in the vicinity of our camp. It was quite a curiosity, suggestive of the time when it was sent on its murderous errand, eight months before. We were pleasantly situated here, and enjoyed ourselves.

Just after our arrival here, two sutlers commenced visiting us, and in the absence of competition, charged exorbitant prices. One day seeing a large crowd around one of the teams, I went up. Found the owner busy selling oranges at ten cents apiece, and cider at ten cents a glass. Apples in the same proportion. And while delivering from the front of the wagon, the soldiers, unbe-known to him, at the same time had tapped a barrel in the rear, and were doing a brisk business, filling canteens, &c. Soon after I heard an uproar, and was just in time to see his wagon tipped over, and his groceries distributed. Knowing the other sutler was in camp with gingerbread, the price of which was twenty-five cents for three pieces, about the size of my hand, I felt anxious to learn his fate. I had not long to wait, as I soon saw one side of a wagon rise in the air, the owner jump from it, and gingerbread flying in all directions. This had a tendency to lower the prices, and since then no outrages of the kind have been perpetrated, as it has not been necessary to repeat the experiment.

CHAPTER 9

A Fracas

How often at home, when with the toil and care incident upon the life of those who "earn their bread by the sweat of the brow," have we as Saturday night approached, and with it the labours of the week were to cease, looked forward to a day of rest. A thousand miles from home, the plough exchanged for the sword, the awl for the bayonet, in the face of a desperate enemy, and the thing is changed.

The Sabbath comes as at home, but unfortunately, is more "honoured in the breach than the observance," and seems to be a day specially appointed by military authorities, for fighting and marching. We received marching orders Saturday, 2nd, and were to be in readiness to march the following morning. As is usual with us the night before a march, all was bustle and confusion. Some were busy packing their effects, others talking, each man having to express his opinion as to where we were to go, the chances for a fight, &c. Another portion, who at other times deny themselves, were indulging in liquor, the result of which was a general howling, extending into the small hours of the night.

The night before our march from Lexington, a portion of the men went to the city, had a plenty to drink, and some of them returned with canteens filled. The consequence was, a riotous night, and but little sleep was to be had. The men quarrelled among themselves, and to cap the climax, at two in the morning, one of the men from the company adjoining, visited Company

F, and indulged in a little shillalah practice. Swinging to the right and left, much to the discomfiture of one of our men, who received a blow on the top of his head, which, judging from the sound, might have felled an ox. He was rendered *hors de combat*, and taken to the surgeon; and after this salutary lesson, the boys thinking best to keep still, we got a few hours sleep. The noisy ones of Company F were christened "lions." The name originated in Camp Casey, where they occupied two of our Sibley tents, on the left of the line, and by their continual howling, made "night hideous."

Saturday, May 2nd, at nightfall, the uproar commenced as usual. At ten I turned in. I kept napping, waking, and sleeping by turns, until two in the morning. At this time, a party in front of my tent were having an altercation which threatened to terminate in a fight. I thought best to see what was going on. Looking out of my hotel, I saw J. R., the same individual who officiated at Lexington, with club raised, threatening to lay it about the ears of his opponent, who was daring him to come on. Friends interfered, preventing them from coming to blows, and after a bad amount of cursing and hard talk, during which the whole regiment were disturbed, they were separated, and quiet reigned again. The immediate results of this night's carousal, were visible to all in the person of one of our drummers, who had indulged beyond his strength, and was found lifeless in his tent, the morning of the 3rd, having "shuffled off this mortal coil" in the melee.

The morning of the 3rd of May found us busy, preparing for the march, regardless of the storm, which was evidently about to open upon us. At eight we were on our way. It commenced raining slightly before we left camp, and after our first rest outside of Richmond at ten, a.m., it commenced in earnest. We hurried on, and at one, p.m., were encamped at Point Lick Creek, having marched a distance of thirteen miles in four hours. Some of the time while on this march, the rain poured in torrents, and we reached camp thoroughly soaked. Soon after our arrival the sun came out, the clouds passed away, and we had a pleasant afternoon. This gave us a chance to roll and tumble upon the grass, dry ourselves, and put up tents at our leisure.

Our camp was situated on the road which runs from Richmond to Lancaster, and was about midway between the two places. It was evident our stay here would be short, as the usual care in laying out camps was not observed here, our tents being pitched in all conceivable ways. Our general formed his headquarters some twenty rods east of our camp, close by a church. This edifice had been built but a short time, was small, of modern style, without a steeple, and very much resembled a New England school-house.

From the time of our arrival here, up to Saturday the 9th, the weather was very disagreeable. Considerable rain fell, and for six days we were enveloped in clouds and fog. But in spite of all this, our general and his staff had frequent visits from the fair ones of Richmond, whose acquaintance they formed during our short sojourn there. They came in groups of half a dozen at a time. The band was called on to serenade the fair visitors, who forming with our officers upon the green in front of the church, joined in the mazy dance, and "tripped the light fantastic toe."

Chapter 10

Enemy on the Cumberland

Sunday, the 10th, at three o'clock in the morning, we again received orders to march. At eight, a.m., the brigade was moving in the direction of Lancaster. Our company this time were detailed as rear guard, and having to wait until all the teams were under way, did not start until ten, a.m. The day was very warm, but having the advantage, as guard, of stopping often, we made an easy march of it. At two, p.m., we arrived in sight of our camp; the brigade encamping upon a hill, within one-half mile of the village of Lancaster—a situation commanding a view of the country for many miles around.

A source of amusement heretofore denied us, we had the privilege of indulging in here. A small pond in the same enclosure with our camp, abounded in fish, some of which, when full grown, reach the enormous weight of one-fourth of a pound. Hooks and lines were in demand, and piscatorial pursuits were the order of the day.

The Twelfth Regiment in white gloves, through the generosity of our Sutler!—Three cheers for H. S. Patterson!—On the afternoon of May 18th, each man was called in front of his orderly's tent, and received a pair, and at dress parade the Twelfth were encased in white gloves. Some suggested the old saying that "puss in gloves catches no mice." From our improved appearance others prophesied the speedy downfall of the rebellion. Much querying occurred in the regiment, about this time, as to when our term of service would expire. One of our men claiming his time as up, it being nine months since his enlistment, hoping to find out when the regiment were to start for home, went to the colonel and thus accosted him:

"Well, Colonel, I suppose my time is out."

Says the colonel, "What are you going to do about it; are you going home now, or are you going to wait for the rest of the boys?"

Says the fellow, somewhat abashed, "I think I will go home with the rest of the boys."

"Well," says the "old colonel," "I guess you had better; we are all going home pretty soon."

The fellow retired, much chop-fallen at the result of his interview.

May 20, at dress parade, was read to us the farewell address of General Naglee, who had resigned his command and was about to return home. He was suffering from an affection of the heart, and found himself unable to continue longer in the field. He was to leave us the 21st, and extended an invitation to all of us to call on him. The evening of the 20th, at sunset, the band formed in front of his quarters, commenced playing, and in a short time a good portion of the brigade assembled, to hear the parting words of the general. We found him sitting in front of his tent, rising occasionally to salute the officers as they came in groups from the different regiments.

The band played a few pieces, when the general, stepping in front, addressed them a few parting words, then, taking them each by the hand, he bade them adieu. Then turning to the soldiers, he made them a short speech, bidding them farewell, saying he would be glad to shake hands with all who chose to come forward. The band played "Home, Sweet Home," at the conclusion of which we all retired to our quarters.

Colonel Griffin, of the Sixth New Hampshire, succeeded General Naglee in the command of the brigade at this time.

May 21st, the enemy were accumulating on the Cumberland, and occupied the south bank of the river, where their movements were closely watched by our forces. Some few days before, they had contrived to throw a force across. This brought on a fight, in which they were repulsed and driven back. We were under marching orders at the time, and held ourselves in readiness to march at short notice in the event it should have been found necessary to have sent reinforcements.

May 22nd, at nine in the evening, we received orders to march. At seven the next morning, the first brigade were on the march, accompanied by the second, who followed close in the rear. Taking the Somerset road, we were soon fairly established in all the privileges and comforts of a march on a hot, dry, dusty day. At eleven, a.m., we stopped for dinner, having marched nine miles. We started again at half-past two, p.m., and at four, p.m., encamped near Crab Orchard, twelve miles from our late camp, near Lancaster.

Chapter 11

Morgan's Cavalry

Upon our marching from Lancaster, one of my acquaintances, whom I thought from his intercourse with the officers might know our destination, informed me that we were to march but three or four miles, and were to encamp in an oak grove. The spot had been selected the day before by our general, and was indeed a beautiful place, abounding in excellent springs of water, and in the immediate vicinity of a river, an admirable place for bathing, &c. It was a very warm day, and as the roads were dry and dusty it made our march unusually severe, and instead of the oak grove, but four miles distant, with all its beautiful surroundings, we made a march of twelve miles, and found ourselves at last located in a thicket of briers, one and a half miles north of the village of Crab Orchard, a spot devoid of everything green, if we except blackberry bushes and pennyroyal, and abounding in all manner of creeping things.

The evening of the 25th, information having been received that the enemy were in the neighbourhood of Somerset, and might make a raid in our direction, we were ordered to be on the alert. Company I was detailed for extra picket duty, and all precaution taken against an attack. The afternoon of the 26th, at six o'clock, the Twelfth struck tents, and moved forward one-half mile beyond the village of Crab Orchard, to the support of the Second New York Battery, which had taken position the night before in a field commanding the Mount Vernon and Somerset roads, which meet at this place. Here we encamped again for a short period.

June the 1st we received orders to put ourselves in light marching condition, and hold ourselves in readiness to march at short notice. Accordingly, the morning of June 2nd, all boxes and barrels available were scraped up, and overcoats, and all other superfluous luggage, was packed and sent to the rear. Many of the boys had flattered themselves that our fighting days were over, but since this last order, begin to think that the "end is not yet."

The evening of June the 3rd, at "dress parade," our colonel made a speech, wherein he congratulated the Twelfth, telling them that in all probability they would again soon have a chance to meet the enemy on a fair field. He hoped to have the privilege of leading them again, and had no doubt they would acquit themselves with credit, and return home an honour to the State they represent. In a short speech of ten minutes we were all impressed with the certainty of a conflict near, and in our imagination could almost hear the din of battle and see the "bloody 12th," eager for the fray, rush into the thickest of the fight, driving all before them.

Soon victory crowns our efforts, and descending from the heavens, the eagle, the emblem of our nationality, perches upon our banner! Our history is to become immortal! Laurel wreaths encircle our brows! Roses shower down upon us, and in the whirling mists, an everlasting halo of glory encompasseth us. Rumour said that our colonel was about to issue to every man in his regiment a tunic, something after the manner of a butcher's frock, and throwing aside every other article of clothing, we were to start at once, and annihilate the enemy in his strongholds. The evening of June 4th we received orders to be in readiness to march the following morning, at half-past four, each man to be provided with sixty rounds of ammunition, and eight days' rations.

At five o'clock the next morning the regiment were in line, and in fifteen minutes we were passing through the village of Crab Orchard, taking the Lancaster road, accompanied by the rest of the brigade. At ten, a.m., when within one mile of Lancaster, we turned aside, and halted until half-past two, p.m. Here it became generally known that we were to march to Nicholasville, as soon as possible, there to find transportation to some place as yet unknown to us. Various were the surmises as to where we were to go. We soon became convinced that the first brigade were to report at Vicksburg. Then the question arose, would the Twelfth accompany them, or be detached and dropped on the way.

At half-past two, p.m., we were ordered into line again; at three passed through Lancaster, and at seven arrived at "Camp Dick Robinson," having marched twenty-one miles. Here we encamped for the night. The appearance of the sky betokened rain, consequently many of us took pains to pitch our tents. This, together with making coffee and eating supper, occupied our time until ten o'clock. About this time we turned in, to gain what little rest we could before "reveille," which was ordered to be beaten at four o'clock in the morning. At the appointed time, the roll of the drums announced to us that our sleeping hours were up. We turned out in haste, having barely time to eat breakfast and pack up before we were called into line.

At half-past four we were on our way again. At seven, a.m., entered Pleasant Valley. Here the scenery became most wild and picturesque, and as we crossed Hickman's Bridge the grandeur of the scenery impressed me beyond anything I have ever witnessed. Mountains, hundreds of feet in height, towered above our heads, in all directions. The bridge is a fine structure; it was built in 1836, is perhaps two hundred feet in length, and spans the Kentucky River, some sixty feet above its waters.

After emerging from this defile, and when within one mile of Nicholasville, Colonel Griffin received a dispatch detaching us from the brigade, with orders for Colonel Browne to report in another direction. At this time we were in advance of the brigade. We immediately came to a halt, and as the brigade passed by, we gave each regiment three parting cheers, and commenced to retrace our steps. After going half a mile we filed to the right, into a grove, where we passed the night.

At five o'clock in the morning we were drummed into line, and on the tenth day of June encamped in Somerset, having marched, in six consecutive days, over one hundred miles, under a broiling sun, with knapsacks heavily laden with rations and ammunition, finding ourselves at last twenty-eight miles from Crab Orchard, the place from whence we started June the 4th. Our encampment was in a grove, quarter of a mile west of the village, on ground occupied by Zollicoffer in 1861; here he prepared to make a stand against the forces sent to repel him; trenches were dug, and large, noble trees, cut at the time, lay thick upon the ground. His fate was decided at Mill Springs, January 20th, 1862.

Nothing of note occurred during our stay here, most of our time being taken up in fighting flies, which swarmed about our camp, and in trying to make ourselves as comfortable as we could under the circumstances. It was extremely warm during our sojourn here, and the flies seemed determined to annihilate us.

June the 20th, at noon, received marching orders again, and at four, p.m., encamped on the heights which form the banks of the Cumberland River, in the immediate vicinity of Stigall's Ferry, seven miles from Somerset. Having a desire to bathe in the waters of this celebrated stream, I visited it for that purpose early the next morning, and returned to camp just in time to take my place in line on our return march. We reached Somerset at one, p.m., rested until three, when we took up our line of march for Jamestown, whither we had been ordered. We encamped for the night on "Logan's Old Fields," where the battle of Mill Springs was fought, January, 1862. This place is distant from Somerset nine miles, which made our day's march sixteen miles. Here we found the 32nd Kentucky, Lieutenant-Colonel Morrow, who had started from Somerset in advance of us, and who were to be our companions to Jamestown, the two regiments to be under the command of Colonel G. H. Browne, the senior officer.

At five, a.m., the following morning, the 32nd took the lead, followed immediately by the 12th. This day we reached Shady Creek, at eight, p.m., where we encamped, having made a march of sixteen miles over the roughest roads imaginable.

At twelve, m., the next day, we passed through Jamestown, and encamped in the immediate vicinity, having marched ten miles over a road where it required the activity and ingenuity of a red ferret to keep us on our feet. June the 24th our teams started for Lebanon, sixty miles distant, to procure rations, and it soon became evident we were not to remain idle here. Our scouts reported the enemy as attempting to cross the Cumberland, and our whole force was employed to hold them in check. Our brave colonel went to the village and ground up his sabre, preparatory to cutting and slashing. A large force was sent out three miles on the road towards Columbia, where a rude fort was constructed and garrisoned, under the supervision of our colonel. Bodies of men were sent in other directions to fell trees, and otherwise obstruct the roads; and all things were made ready to give the enemy a warm reception.

June the 28th, Colonel Woolford's Cavalry and Colonel Kautz's Brigade joined us, since which time there has been constant skirmishing with Morgan's advance. Our regiment at this time saw hard service. Heavy pickets were kept out all the time; our rations were giving out, and, to make it more disagreeable, it rained continually every day, some of the time pouring in torrents. Our teams, that were expected the 28th, were unfortunately delayed on their return by the presence of the enemy in Columbia.

They had passed Green River Bridge, and were hurrying along, and had nearly reached Columbia, before they were aware of the danger; upon learning which, they immediately hurried back across Green River, when meeting a force of thirty men, sent from Lebanon to protect them, they concluded to make a stand here until morning. In the course of the night, the bridge was carried away by the freshet, caused by the heavy rains. There was no other alternative left them, but to reach camp by a circuitous route, crossing the river at a ford some twenty miles to the north. July 3rd, when within ten miles of camp, they were attacked by sixty or seventy of Morgan's Cavalry.[1] The guard showing themselves equal to the emergency, dashed among them with great fury, repulsing them, killing one, and taking seven of them prisoners; the rest made good their escape.

Shortly after, the teams reached Jamestown, much excited by their adventurous trip. Meanwhile we were expecting to be attacked, and were twice called into line. The morning of July 4th quite a force of the enemy came close upon us; the signal howitzers were fired, and the long roll was beaten. The regiment turned out, took position, and awaited their approach; but the enemy avoided us. Sunday, the 5th, it becoming known that Morgan with his whole force had crossed the river, and slipped past us, we were ordered back to Somerset. At nine a.m., the stores were put aboard the teams, and we took up our line of march.

It was a very warm, sultry day, and the roads were in bad condition, owing to the late rains, making our march extremely difficult. The poor boys were sore pressed, and tents and blankets flew in all directions. We reached Russell's Spring and made a halt there until four, p.m. We had twenty-five prisoners with us, the fruit of our excursion to Jamestown. At four, we started, when it commenced to rain and kept it up till dark; much of the time it poured in torrents, and we made a march of eight miles, with only two halts, of five minutes' each, and at dark encamped one mile from Shady Creek, soaked to the skin.

The next morning, July 6th, we waited until nine, a.m., for the team to come up with us, when we started again, marched eleven miles, and again halted for the night. July 7th, reached Somerset at seven, p.m.

The next day, at five, p.m., marched again, *en route* for Hickman's Bridge, by way of Crab Orchard and Stanford. Marched six miles, and halted for the night. July 9th, marched twenty-two miles, reaching Crab Orchard at eight, p.m.

The next day passed through Stanford at ten, and halted for

---

1. *History of Morgan's Cavalry* by Basil. W. Duke also published by Leonaur.

dinner one mile from the village at eleven, a.m. Here our colonel was told he could give his regiment a ride on the supply train, which was all ready to go to Hickman's Bridge. Our colonel accepted the offer, and in one-half hour we were aboard and on our way, much to the relief of the suffering, sore-footed members of the Rhode Island "Itinerant" Regiment. The train made a halt at Dick River, and we dismounted and encamped. The next day, July the 11th, at one, p.m., we dismounted at Hickman's Bridge, marched up the hill, and at two, p.m., halted at General Burnside's head-quarters, for orders. Here we remained until nine, a.m., July the 12th, when we got orders to report in Cincinnati. We then marched to Nicholasville, went aboard the train at two, p.m., and at eleven at night arrived in Covington.

On the 13th, at seven, a.m., we crossed the Ohio, and stacking arms in front of the Fifth Street Market House, waited there for breakfast. Here we learned that the omnipresent Morgan was within a few miles of the city, and advancing. Martial law was to take effect in the city at ten, a.m. Companies were arming and organizing, and we were soon informed that nothing but the presence of the Twelfth Rhode Island Volunteers would save the city from utter destruction. This pleasing bit of information was imparted to us after dinner, while labouring to get up Vine Street Hill, to a new camp where we were destined to remain for a few days longer. This was sorry news, and some of the boys were rather riotous over it, the thought naturally suggesting itself to them, whether the same necessity might not exist in Bungtown or in any other place. By the way, the term of service for which our regiment was mustered in, had already expired; and the Twelfth Rhode Island Volunteers, weary and worn out, had hoped that we were finally on our way home.

It was indeed disheartening to many of us, who had expected that upon our arrival here nothing would occur to interrupt our journey. Little did we think that even here in Ohio the presence of John Morgan would render it necessary for us to rally again. About this time, also, the New York riot was raging, and some apprehension was felt by the authorities of a similar demonstration in Cincinnati. This was enough to detain us, and at the junction of the two roads on Mount Auburn, on the afternoon of the 13th day of July, the Twelfth Rhode Island Volunteers established their camp, and on the same evening the "redoubtable John" illuminated it by burning a bridge within three miles of us.

Sunday, the 19th, reinforcements having arrived, we were relieved, and at seven o'clock, a.m., of that day we left Cincinnati for Rhode Island; where, on the 29th day of July, 1863, we were mustered from the service of the United States. The particulars of our journey, together with our reception in Providence, I copy from the *Providence Evening Press* of July 22nd, at the conclusion of which is appended the Order which General Burnside, in appreciation of our services, upon our leaving his Department, issued to the regiment.

RETURN OF THE TWELFTH REGIMENT.

This noble regiment returned home today from its arduous and protracted services at the seat of war. The unusual amount of hardship and exposure to which it has been subjected, the important duties it has performed, and the heavy losses it has sustained in the defence of the country, made it highly appropriate that it should be received with demonstrations expressive of the popular interest in all that concerns our brave soldiers.

The record of this regiment will compare favourably with that of any nine months regiment which has been in the service during the war. In addition to long and frequent marches, they have spent seven months of their time at the front, in the face of danger, and where the duties imposed upon them have taxed their every energy to the utmost.

The regiment left Cincinnati on Sunday morning, and proceeded by rail to Dunkirk on the Erie Railroad, and thence to New York, where they arrived at eleven o'clock yesterday morning. They started about one o'clock for Providence on the steamer Commodore, arriving about four o'clock a short distance below Nayatt, where they anchored. They came up to the city shortly afterward, and landed about seven o'clock. A salute was fired by the Marine Artillery.

The Fourth and Sixth Regiments Rhode Island Militia were drawn up on Benefit Street to receive the returning veterans, and loudly cheered them as they passed through the opened lines. A crowd of expectant friends, who had assembled at the Point, immediately gathered around the gallant boys, and the short halt was improved in the interchange of the heartiest greetings.

About eight o'clock the line of march was formed in the following order:—

American Brass Band.

Drum Corps.

Section of Marine Artillery.

Sixth Regiment, R. I. M., Col. James H. Armington.

Drum Corps.

Fourth Regiment, R. I. M., Col. Nelson Viall.

Drum Corps.

Twelfth Regiment, R. I.V., Col. George H. Browne, Lieut. Col. James Shaw, Jr., Major Cyrus G. Dyer,

Adjutant Matthew N. Chappell.

Co. B, Capt. James M. Longstreet, Lieuts. Albert W. Delanah and Charles A. Winchester.

Co. I, Capt. George A. Spink, Lieuts. Munson H. Najac and John H. Weaver.

Co. F, Capt. William E. Hubbard, Lieuts. William H. King and Francisco Ballou.

Co. K, Capt. Oscar Lapham, Lieuts. Edmund W. Fales and Charles H. Potter.

Co. E, (colour company,) Capt. John J. Phillips, Lieuts. Luther Cole, Jr., and Edward V. Wescott.

Co. D, Capt. John P. Abbott, Lieuts. George H. Tabor and Henry M. Tillinghast.

Co. H, Capt. Oliver H. Perry, Lieuts. Arnold F. Salisbury

and J. N. Williams.

Co. A, Capt. Christopher H. Alexander, Lieuts. Edward F. Bacon and Joseph C. Whiting, Jr.

Co. G, Capt. William C. Rogers, Lieuts. James A. Bowen and Fenner H. Peckham, Jr.

Co. C, Capt. James H. Allen, Lieuts. George Bucklin and Beriah G. Browning.

Quartermaster, John L. Clarke; Surgeon, Benoni Carpenter; Assist. Surgeon, Samuel M. Fletcher; Chaplain, S. W. Field.

Rear guard of twenty men detailed from all the companies.

The procession marched over the usual route to Exchange Place, where the men stacked arms, and universal hand-shakings and congratulations were the order of the day.

The streets were lined with people. Flags were hung out all along the line of march; handkerchiefs were waving everywhere, and bouquets and wreaths were scattered with a liberal hand. The regiments doing escort duty turned out with very full ranks, and made a most effective demonstration.

A fine collation, served by L. H. Humphreys, was provided for the troops in Howard Hall. There were eight tables running the entire length of the room, neatly spread with most acceptable fare, and presenting a most cheerful and inviting appearance. The officers of the regiments were entertained upon the platform. About two thousand plates were laid, and all three of the regiments were amply provided for.

The Rev. Dr. Swain, Chaplain of the Sixth Regiment, invoked a blessing upon the repast, after which His Excellency Governor Smith came forward, and in a very happy manner welcomed the regiment back to the State and thanked them for the services they had rendered in the field.

Colonel Browne responded substantially as follows:

In my own behalf, and that of the officers and soldiers under my command, I thank you for the kind manner in which you have been pleased to speak of us. Next to the approbation of our own consciences we prize most highly the approbation of those we love. That approbation of conscience we enjoy. To the utmost of our ability since we left this State, we have endeavoured to uphold her honour, and to labour for the suppression of the rebellion. We prize this reception as an evidence of your approval.

Your words of praise show that our services have not been unmarked. Still it may be well for me to advert briefly to some facts in our history as a regiment. We have travelled over 3,500 miles, five hundred of which has been on foot, literally carrying the houses we lived in, the provisions upon which we were to subsist for six and even eight days, and the arms with which we were to defend ourselves and oppose the enemy.

On the field of Fredericksburg one hundred and nine of my brave men were lost to my command. Afterwards, when pestilence stalked through the camp, and amid hardship and privation, one hundred and twenty more were swept away in three short weeks; not all indeed to the silent grave, since a few still linger in hospitals.

But through the constant efforts of my officers to preserve cleanliness and discipline in the camp, we are happy in bringing back to our friends today over seven hundred of those who marched with me from Washington to the banks of the Rappahannock.

Our duties have been of the most varied kind. But through them all the uniform kindness of the State has at all times watched over us. While we were in camp where pestilence assailed us and want made us suffer, your good ship *Elizabeth and Helen* brought us much needed supplies; and if your bounty burdened our backs, it certainly lightened our hearts and cheered us on the weary march.

Let me in conclusion congratulate you, the officers who surround you, and all our citizens, that we arrive at home at a time when everything is so cheering and prosperous. Gentlemen, nine short months more, and you will see this country a reunited country—a mighty nation, whose arms will be more a shield for every citizen than was ever Rome in her proudest days.

At the conclusion of the collation, the military were dismissed. The Twelfth Regiment were ordered to reassemble in this city on Wednesday next, at ten o'clock, a.m.

Headquarters, Department of the Ohio,
Cincinnati, Ohio, July 17, 1863.
General Orders, No. 115.

On the departure of the Twelfth Regiment Rhode Island Volunteers, at the expiration of their term of enlistment, the Commanding General wishes to express his regret at taking leave of soldiers who, in their brief service, have become veterans. After passing through experiences of great hardship and danger, they will return with the proud satisfaction that, in the ranks of their country's defenders, the reputation of their State has not suffered in their hands.

By command of Maj. Gen. Burnside.
Lewis Richmond,
Assist. Adjutant-General.

Reminiscences of Service with the Twelfth Rhode Island Volunteers

Pardon E. Tillinghast

Contents

Reminiscences of Service with the Twelfth Rhode Island Volunteers

The months of July, August, September and October of 1862, were stirring times in Rhode Island,—and in fact throughout the entire North. The vigorous onward movement of our army towards Richmond, which had been long and frequently promised, was still deferred. The decisive victory won by the Union forces over Lee's army at Malvern Hills at great cost, which, in the judgment of every officer in the Army of the Potomac save one, and he the chief, should have been immediately followed by a determined advance towards the rebel stronghold, which was only about a day's march distant, was supplemented by the now somewhat stereotyped order to "fall back," thus presenting the not altogether inspiring military spectacle of a victorious army running away from its defeated and thoroughly demoralized enemy.

General Pope's campaign in Northern Virginia, inaugurated with a great flourish of trumpets, had resulted disastrously; the rebel army was greatly encouraged by the inactivity and the vacillating conduct of their opponents, and had commenced a vigorous aggressive movement. The National capital was again in imminent peril, causing a feverish excitement throughout the country; Baltimore and Cincinnati were seriously threatened, and a great crisis was evidently at hand. Vigorous measures must be adopted at once, or our boasted Republic would soon be a thing of the past.

The president, in view of the great emergency, had ordered

drafts, amounting in the aggregate to six hundred thousand men, one-half thereof for three years, and the other half for nine months, the latter to be drawn from the enrolled militia; and the utmost activity everywhere prevailed in connection with the raising, equipping and forwarding of this vast army of recruits.

Rhode Island was thoroughly alive to the occasion, determined not to be outdone by any of her sister States in meeting this new and pressing demand upon her loyalty and her resources; and meeting it too, if possible, without resort to a draft, which, of course, was obnoxious to the sentiments of the people. In order to promote enlistments, the stores in some places were closed at 3 p. m. each day; war meetings were held every evening, and the greatest enthusiasm was manifested. The whole State seemed to be one vast recruiting camp, and all the people, both male and female, to be engaged in the business. For it should ever be remembered, to the praise of the women of Rhode Island, that they were fully as loyal and as devoted to our country's cause during the rebellion, as were the men; and that in very many cases they suffered and sacrificed quite as much at home, though in different ways, as did their husbands and sons and brothers in the field.

In such a state of public feeling what could I, a young unmarried man, do consistent with a fair amount of self-respect but enlist? Evidently nothing; and so I left the teacher's desk and enlisted as a private in Company C, Eleventh Rhode Island Volunteers, under Captain Charles W. Thrasher. I was detailed for service in the quartermaster's department under Lieutenant John L. Clark, and shortly after was transferred with him (I never knew why) to the Twelfth, and was appointed by Colonel Browne to the office of Quartermaster Sergeant.

Camp Stevens, in Providence, was a lively place during the latter part of September and the first part of October, 1862. The Eleventh and Twelfth regiments were both encamped there together during a part of this time, preparatory to their departure for the seat of war. The former left on Monday, October sixth, and the latter on Tuesday, October twenty-first.

The Twelfth Regiment was composed mainly of good Rhode Island material, and was officered by intelligent, patriotic and brave-hearted men. There were representatives from nearly all of the ordinary walks and callings of life, thus furnishing the command with facilities for almost any emergency; and it was proverbial that whatever could be done by anybody could be done by someone in this regiment. The officers and the privates were well disposed towards each other; there was a prevalent spirit of prompt obedience to orders; and in general a manifest disposition on the part of all to make themselves useful and serviceable both to the Government and to each other.

A journey of seventy-seven hours from Providence, partly by rail, partly by water, and partly on foot, brought this newly-formed regiment to Camp Chase, which was situated across the Potomac from Washington, in the neighborhood of Arlington Heights. The work of pitching our tents was at once commenced and rapidly pushed forward. But before it was completed, a violent storm of wind and rain broke upon us which continued for nearly two days without intermission. And such a storm! I think I never saw the like before or since. It did not simply rain, but it came down in great broad sheets of water; it poured; it came in great gusts. And then the wind—it whirled, it roared, it got upon its giant legs, and fairly howled with rage as the weary hours of that first night in camp wore away.

And such a sorry sight as that camp presented the next morning was not calculated to promote one's military enthusiasm, to say the least. Many of the tents, all of which had been hastily erected, had been blown down during the night, and the drenched and shivering inmates were wandering about in search of shelter or assistance in again erecting their uncertain habitations. Baggage and camp equipage were scattered in all directions, and confusion held high carnival generally. As if this were not enough for beginners, we were also treated to our first installment of Virginia mud, which covered the entire surface of the ground to a depth of two or three inches. No description of this unique article, however, is necessary here. It is perhaps needless to say that our first impressions of a soldier's life in the "Sunny South" were not altogether favorable.

But this storm, like all others, came to an end, and the bright, warm sunshine, together with the diligence of many busy hands, soon repaired most of the damage; so that the regiment was able to appear on brigade review in gallant style, on Tuesday, the twenty-eighth of October, the fourth day after our arrival, before the venerable General Casey, in whose division it had been brigaded.

One week was the length of our stay at Camp Chase, at the end of which brief period we folded our tents and made a "Sabbath day's journey," although somewhat longer than that permitted by the Jewish economy on that sacred day, to Fairfax Seminary. (I may remark in passing that perhaps not the most scrupulous regard was had by most of the commanders who conducted the operations of our armies, either to the Jewish or Christian economy concerning the Sabbath day). This proved to be a charming location, indeed. The land was high, overlooking the broad Potomac for a long distance; the city of Alexandria, situated two miles to the south, was in full view, while in the distance on our left was the magnificent dome of the capitol at Washington.

The land sloped in a broad, undulating sweep towards the Potomac in front of us; the large and dignified brick buildings of Fairfax Seminary, then used as a hospital, were situated just to the north, in the rear, surrounded by a stately grove of trees (which, sad to say, speedily succumbed to the soldier's axe); several fine country residences were scattered about in the immediate vicinity, evidently the recent homes of affluence and luxury, but now abandoned to the tender mercies of strangers in arms, being used mainly by general and field officers, with their staffs, for headquarters.

And although their owners were rebels fighting against the Government, I must, nevertheless, confess to a strong feeling of sympathy which I then had for them, and thousands like them, in the untold and untellable distress, privation and suffering which they and their families must have experienced in being driven as exiles from their homes and firesides, their property appropriated to the use of their enemies, and what they, in the main, honestly considered their inalienable rights, taken from them. But such is and will continue to be the fate of war.

Regiments of soldiers were on every side of us. A few rods in front was the Fifteenth Connecticut, Colonel Wright; in the rear was the Thirteenth New Hampshire, Colonel Stevens; on the right the Twenty-seventh New Jersey, Colonel Mindil; and on the left a stalwart regiment of "six footers" from Maine; while for a mile or more in all directions little else was visible but camps of soldiers. Truly this was a "tented field." Everything about our new camp, which was named Camp Casey, was soon put in the best of order, cleanliness and good order being prime virtues with Colonel Browne, and always being strenuously insisted on.

Our company was detailed each day at first for picket duty on the long line at the front near Cloud's Mills, which was about five miles distant; but subsequently the entire regiment performed this duty for twenty-four hours at a time, alternating with the other regiments of the brigade. The regiment was diligently perfecting itself in the manual of arms, and a military air and bearing were everywhere apparent. We had now commenced soldiering in good earnest. My principal duties, under the direction of the quartermaster, were to see that the commissary department was kept constantly supplied with everything in the way of subsistence which the army regulations allowed. Washington and Alexandria were the great reservoirs of these supplies, and to one or the other of these places I went three or four times a week, accompanied by two or more four mule teams, with which to haul the stores to camp.

The great army bakery was in the basement of the capitol building, whither we went for our supply of bread. And I think I do not exaggerate by saying that I have seen a line of army wagons half a mile or more in length, each awaiting its turn to be filled with the nice brown loaves. I need hardly say that after leaving the vicinity of Washington we bade an enforced good-bye to soft bread.

On one of my journeys to Alexandria, after getting my teams loaded with rations, I took a stroll about the somewhat anti-quated city, visiting places of interest, amongst which was the Marshall House, where the brave Colonel Ellsworth met his ter-rible fate, and from which house the entire banisters of the stairs which he ascended in going to the roof to haul down a rebel flag, had been carried away piecemeal by visitors, as mementoes of the tragic event. Other parts of the building had also been sadly mutilated for the same purpose. But the stars and stripes had permanently supplanted the rebel flag hauled down by the lamented Ellsworth, and were proudly floating from that now historic building.

I also visited another place of interest, but with what different feelings I will not attempt to relate. It was a large block which bore the following prominent sign: "Price, Birch & Co., Dealers in Slaves." Connected with it was a huge pen to hold the slaves, and an auction block from which thousands doubtless had been bought and sold. But for this establishment and what it repre-sented, neither the tragic scene at the Marshall House nor the gigantic military operations then going on from one end of the country to the other, would ever have been witnessed.

I was also mail-carrier for the regiment to and from the post office in Alexandria, and was always cheerfully received on my return with a heavy mail; for amongst the chief delights of a soldier was a letter from home. As there was no salary attached to this branch of the mail service I was not accused of offensive partisanship, but permitted to hold the office to the end of my term of enlistment.

November 27, 1862, was recognized by us as Thanksgiving day, although the turkey, without which no Yankee can prop-erly observe the day, was conspicuous only by its absence. The usual amusements of the occasion, however, including a sack race between two men, each enveloped in a bed-sack drawn up and tied under his chin, were engaged in and greatly enjoyed.

The governor's proclamation was read by Chaplain Field, and appropriate religious services were conducted by him in front of headquarters.

As it had been currently rumored for some time that Camp Casey was to be our winter quarters, the boys had taken great pains to make their habitations as snug and cosy as possible for the rapidly approaching cold weather. The non-commissioned staff, of which I was a member, appropriated to their use a roof-less negro hut in the rear of the stately old mansion house which was occupied by the colonel and staff for headquarters, and by using the fly of a large tent for a roof, and otherwise improving it, we converted it into very comfortable quarters, anticipating quite a jolly time therein during the winter. The mess consisted of Sergeant Major Daniel R. Ballou, subsequently promoted to the office of lieutenant for bravery at the Battle of Fredericksburg; Commissary Sergeant Amasa F. Eddy; Quartermaster's Clerk Erastus Richardson; the quartermaster sergeant, and William, the colored boy.

But alas for all plans which have no firmer base than rumors in the army. For the regiment had no more than fully settled down to housekeeping for the winter, when, on Sunday, November thirtieth, orders were received that Colonel Wright's brigade, of which the Twelfth Rhode Island was a part, would move to the front the next day at twelve o'clock. As to their destination, no one knew save Colonel Browne, if indeed he did, and, as a matter of course, speculations and conjectures of all sorts were freely indulged in. "Shelter tents" were issued at once, the men were ordered to provide themselves with three days' cooked rations and have everything in readiness to move promptly at the appointed time. Truly, "there was hurrying to and fro, and gathering in hot haste," each one busily making ready for his unknown journey. There was but very little grumbling about leaving our nicely arranged camp and beautiful situation, although we had but very recently received what seemed to be almost a positive promise that these should be our winter quarters.

The baggage was reduced to the lowest marching standard,

and the men ordered to take nothing in their knapsacks except what they actually needed. The consequence was that a large portion of their "traps" had to be left behind, and judging from the number of officers' trunks which I shipped to Rhode Island after the regiment left, I doubt not that more dress uniforms adorned the wardrobes at home than their owners in the field. Such things look exceedingly nice on dress parade or review, but they are not altogether useful on a forced march or in a fight.

The hour of departure having arrived, the companies marched from their several streets, the regimental line was formed, and all was in readiness for a move. I must confess to an almost overwhelming feeling of loneliness as I saw the long soldierly column moving off, led by the splendid band of the Thirteenth New Hampshire, for amongst other things I thought it quite probable that before I should again see them, their ranks might be thinned by the terrible shock of battle. And so, alas! they were. But having received orders from the colonel to remain in charge of the camp, which remained as before, except that its occupants were gone, the tents being all left standing, I had no alternative but to obey.

About seventy men were left in the camp, all of whom, with the exception of the quartermaster's clerk and myself, were on the sick list. Truly this was "a sick house with no doctor," for the surgeon and each of his assistants had gone forward with the regiment. We were cheered, however, just at evening by the return of our kind-hearted assistant surgeon, Doctor Prosper K. Hutchinson, now long since gone to his reward, who was sent back to remain with the sick ones until they should be able to join their comrades. The clerk and myself now appropriated the colonel's somewhat luxurious quarters to our use, and as we had plenty of provisions and a good cook, there was no occasion for us to complain of our fate.

The fourth day after the regiment left, winter set in in good earnest. Snow fell to the depth of several inches, and the weather was bitterly cold and severe. I contrasted my comfortable quarters, as I sat by a blazing wood fire at night, with those of my comrades huddled in shelter tents and shivering from cold, somewhere on their tedious march to the front, and heartily pitied, while I could not alleviate, their condition. With the aid of some of the convalescents I struck the tents, turned over the camp stores and equipage, except a small part which was to go forward to the quartermaster's department in Washington, settled my accounts with the government, and, through the kindness of the quartermaster of the One Hundred and Eleventh New York, who loaned me the use of his teams, hauled the balance of the baggage to Alexandria, placed it on board a boat for Acquia Creek, and on the seventeenth of December took leave of Camp Casey, and with thirteen men went forward to join my regiment.

It was found encamped near General Sumner's headquarters on the heights opposite Fredericksburg, which place I learned it reached after a week's march from Camp Casey, travelling upwards of sixty miles—part of the time through the mud, and part thereof through the snow and over the frozen ground. My friend, Captain Lapham, who experienced the hardships of this never-to-be-forgotten march, has already vividly described it to you in his admirable paper on the Twelfth Rhode Island.

The terrible Battle of Fredericksburg had been fought three days before my arrival at Falmouth, and I knew of it only from others and from the fearful havoc which it had made in the ranks of my comrades, upwards of one-fifth of the entire regiment having been either killed, wounded, or found missing at the close of that sanguinary contest. The part taken by the gallant Twelfth has also been graphically portrayed in the paper just referred to, by one who took an honorable part therein, and it would be presumption in me to attempt a word in addition.

The great Army of the Potomac, now upwards of one hundred thousand strong, was stretched along the eastern bank of the Rappahannock from Falmouth southward to, and including, General Franklin's division, and for miles there was but little space between the regimental camps of this mighty host. Our picket line was on the left bank of the river, while that of the enemy was on the right in plain sight, and for the most part the two lines were within reach of each other's rifles. But there was little firing done, it seeming to be tacitly understood that their principal business was to mutually watch, instead of shoot, each other. Anxious to see how rebels in arms looked, I rode the length of our picket line and inspected them as best I could, from this tolerably safe distance, and became satisfied that a nearer approach was undesirable.

Our base of supplies was Acquia Creek, about fifteen miles in our rear, towards Washington, and thither I had to frequently go for our subsistence. The trains to this place were daily laden with the sick and wounded on their way to the great hospitals in and around Washington. And some of the sights that I saw in connection with the removal of our poor, maimed, sick and dying soldiers, shortly after the terrible battle, would be too painful to relate. I do not mean that they were not as well treated and as kindly cared for as was practicable under the circumstances, but that from their great numbers, the inadequate means for handling them, and the distance over which they had to be transported in crowded box cars and filthy steamboats before much ould be done for them, it was impossible but that their sufferings in many cases should be of the most aggravated character.

Our situation while in front of Fredericksburg was anything but comfortable. The men lived in all sorts of rudely constructed cabins, bough-houses and even subterranean huts, having no tents save the miserable misnamed shelter tents, which were used only as roofs for the conglomerate of structures which their ingenuity had devised. The fireplaces were made of logs cemented and plastered with mud, and the chimneys mainly with empty barrels set on top of each other, (the heads being first knocked out,) and they also cemented together and plastered with mud.

This Virginia mud, when thoroughly dried by the fire, is almost as hard as common brick. The water which we had to use and drink here was simply execrable. I don't think it was so bad as that in the Cove Basin, but it had a very similar appearance. Each little spring and rivulet were eagerly sought and constantly used by continual streams of soldiers, necessarily keeping them in a perturbed and more or less filthy condition; and besides, it was impossible that some portion of the vast amount of offal accumulating from this great army should not find its way into these sources of our water supply. This was specially so when, as frequently happened, several regiments were encamped on the same little stream. Much sickness was caused during our uncomfortable stay here by this detestable water.

On the sixteenth of January, 1863, we received marching orders, but were directed to remain in camp, simply holding ourselves in readiness to move at short notice. The line of march of the right grand division commenced on January nineteenth and was continued through the twentieth. Regiment after regiment, followed by long strings of batteries, continued to move directly past our camp all day long, going to the right. Another great battle was supposed to be imminent. But alas for human plans; whether made by great generals or by persons unknown to fame, they are exceedingly liable to be thwarted.

On the afternoon of the twentieth a cold northeast storm of wind, snow, sleet and rain came on and continued with increasing force for more than thirty-six hours, which necessarily put an end to the strategic movement of General Burnside, for the roads became utterly impassable for the artillery, and practically so for all military purposes. After floundering about in the clayey mire for three days, the brave fellows came tramping back, weary and thoroughly disgusted, and again took up their abode in their wretched old quarters. Our gallant General Burnside was now relieved of the command of the great Army of the Potomac, and General Hooker appointed to succeed him.

On the afternoon of February ninth, we broke camp and took the cars for Acquia Creek, *en route* for Fortress Monroe, as was supposed, but really for Newport News. There was hilarious rejoicing on all hands at the prospect of at last getting away from our abominable quarters. The huts were set on fire; bonfires were made from the great piles of combustible *débris* which had accumulated during the winter; the rude barns which had sheltered our horses and mules added to the conflagration, and for an hour or so before embarking we held high carnival amidst the smoking ruins of "Camp Misery." At Acquia Creek we went on board the transport steamers *Metamora* and *Juniata*, and the next morning steamed down the broad Potomac.

The agreeable change of situation, together with the pleasant sail, were very invigorating, and the men seemed almost to forget that they were soldiers, and to imagine themselves on some holiday excursion. Arriving off Fortress Monroe at four a.m. of the second day out, we awaited orders from General Dix, which being received we proceeded to Newport News and disembarked. We had at last got beyond Virginia mud, though still in Virginia, the soil at this place being light and sandy, and the ground for miles almost as level as Dexter Training Ground.

The schooner *Elizabeth and Helen* from Providence, which we had long been expecting, arrived about the same time. She brought a little more than three hundred boxes from friends at home for our regiment, and our portion of the cargo of vegetables was about ninety barrels. So that, altogether, we had a "right smart heap" of the good things from home. The contents of the boxes being largely of a very perishable nature, were considerably damaged on account of having been so long on the journey. But we made the best of it, and enjoyed the unpacking of those boxes quite as much, without doubt, as our friends at home did the packing. Nothing could have been more beneficial to us than the generous supply of vegetables which we received, having subsisted mainly on salt meats and hard-tack while at Fredericksburg.

"A" tents were here issued to the companies; everything was cheerful and tidy about the camp, and we seemed to be living in a new world. My duties called me to Fortress Monroe nearly every day, which gave me a delightful little sail, together with charming scenery and plenty of work. The scene of the exciting and unequal contest between the *Merrimac* and the *Cumberland*, in Hampton Roads in March, 1862, was immediately in front of us; and about a mile from the shore, in the direction of Norfolk, could be seen a portion of the masts of the latter, emerging from the water.

After a stay of precisely six weeks at Newport News, during which time nothing of very great importance transpired in the Ninth Army Corps, all of which were encamped at this delightful place, the Second Brigade, of which the Twelfth was a part, was ordered to the far-off city of Lexington, Kentucky. Our regiment at once embarked on the steamer *Long Island* for Baltimore, whence we were to go by rail to the West. Some of the scenes on board that steamer at night were ludicrous in the extreme. I have heard of one's "hair standing seven ways for Sunday," of things being "at sixes and sevens," and "all heads and points," but I must aver that the packing of the men on that boat exceeded anything I had ever seen in the way of mixing up human beings. They bestowed themselves in every conceivable position.

It was almost an impossibility to go three steps without causing someone to cry out, "Keep off from me!" or, "O, my fingers!" an oath generally preceding the expression, just for the sake of making it emphatic. The head of a soldier might frequently be seen mixed in with the feet of two or three of his immediate neighbors. And in one case I discovered two men lying directly under one of the horses, fast asleep. I soon ascertained, however, that they had been imbibing too freely of poor whiskey, and that therefore there was probably little immediate danger from their situation.

A sail of sixteen hours brought us to Baltimore, and a ride of three hundred and forty miles over the Baltimore and Ohio Railroad took us to Pittsburgh, Pennsylvania, where we arrived at twelve o'clock on Saturday night, March twenty-eighth, tired and hungry. To our great joy we were immediately invited into the large and beautifully decorated hall occupied by the Soldiers' Relief Society, where we found a splendid supper awaiting us. There were twelve tables, each running the entire length of the hall, each arranged to accommodate one hundred men, and all richly laden with an abundance of delicious food and fruit.

Compliments were few and exceedingly brief, but the rattle of crockery and knives and forks was long and continuous.

The Seventh Rhode Island was in the hall at the same time, and you may be assured that Little Rhody showed an unbroken front here, as she had already done under more trying circumstances elsewhere. Suspended from the front of the platform was the following in large letters: "Pittsburgh Welcomes Her Country's Defenders;" while underneath this was "Roanoke, Newbern, Fredericksburg, Burnside, and the Ninth Army Corps."

After the sumptuous repast was ended, Colonel Browne stepped upon the platform, and in a few appropriate and feeling remarks returned his thanks to the citizens of Pittsburgh for their hospitality to the soldiers of Rhode Island, and closed by proposing three cheers for our benefactors, which were given with a roar that seemed almost to raise the roof. We then marched out to make room for others that were waiting, the remainder of our brigade being nearby. One of the waiters, who, I was informed, was the daughter of one of the first citizens of the city, told me that this hall had not been closed night or day for more than a week, and that every soldier who had passed through the city for a long time had partaken of their bounty if he chose to do so. Nearly five thousand had been fed during the past twelve hours, and still there was an abundance.

At ten a.m. we took the cars for Cincinnati, which we reached after a pleasant ride of about four hundred miles through the most delightful section of country we had yet seen. We almost imagined ourselves making one of "Perham's Grand Excursions to the West." Everywhere along the route we met with tokens of welcome and encouragement. White handkerchiefs fluttered from ten thousand fair hands, while the stars and stripes were displayed "from cottage, hall and tower," in great profusion. At Steubenville, Ohio, I should judge the inhabitants were nearly all at the depot on our arrival, where they greeted us with cheer upon cheer, besides innumerable expressions of loyalty and good will. Five long trains of cars, containing the five regiments of our brigade, kept within a short distance of each other during this entire journey, and when the forward train stopped, the others would come up within a few rods of each other, thus constituting an almost unbroken train for about two miles. The impromptu foraging parties that emerged from each of those trains whenever they came to a brief halt, it is unnecessary to describe to veterans.

The brigade received a perfect ovation at Cincinnati. The streets were crowded with the enthusiastic populace, many buildings were brilliantly illuminated, and the entire conduct of the people proved most conclusively that the Union sentiment here was dominant. While passing along one of the streets our regiment was treated to a perfect shower of nice white handkerchiefs, which were thrown from the windows of a large brick block by a company of ladies. Each of these souvenirs was delicately perfumed and bore the name of the fair donor. We were also treated to another supper here, which, had we not fared so very sumptuously at Pittsburgh, would have been pronounced the ne plus ultra of feasts. After eating till we could eat no more, a fresh supply was brought on with which to fill our empty haversacks for the remainder of the journey.

I was busily occupied all night, in company with a squad of men, in transferring the baggage across the river to Covington in ferry-boats, and loading it on board the train which was to convey us to Lexington, which city we reached the following day, having been six days on the journey from Newport News. We encamped on the State Fair Grounds, west of the city, a spacious and charming location, adorned with elegant shade trees, and surrounded with the stately suburban residences of some of the chivalry of Kentucky. You may perhaps infer that we were somewhat influenced by our aristocratic surroundings when I inform you that while here, our firewood consisted mainly of black-walnut, the ordinary fence-rails in that vicinity being composed of that material.

The Sunday following our arrival here, the regiment was visited and briefly addressed by the venerable General Leslie Coombs, of Kentucky, that staunch and life-long enemy of secession, who was a friend and old acquaintance of Colonel Browne. His tall and manly form, his long, flowing white hair, and his stately bearing, together with his stirring and patriotic remarks in favor of the preservation of the Union and the vigorous prosecution of the war, made an impression upon my mind that I shall never forget.

After a week's sojourn here, our brigade turned its face southward and commenced what subsequently proved to be a long series of marches back and forth across the State, protecting exposed points and preparing for a probable meeting with the rebels either under General Breckenridge or General Morgan, who were constantly menacing the southern borders of the State. And besides, the mountainous districts thereof were infested with marauding bands, mainly under the general direction of Morgan, who were carrying on a guerrilla warfare both against the Unionists of the State, who constituted a majority of all the people, and also against the Union forces stationed there, thus keeping the citizens in a constant state of anxiety and trepidation. The pillaging and murdering of the peaceable and inoffensive citizens of that would-be loyal State by these organized bands of ruffians, constitute to my mind one of the darkest pictures of our civil war.

Twenty-two miles over a macadamized road, through the celebrated "Blue Grass" region, brought us to Winchester, a pleasant inland village in Clarke county, where we were allowed to remain for the full period of eight days. Our next stopping place was at Richmond, a very inviting post-village of about fifteen hundred inhabitants in Madison County, twenty miles south of Winchester. This march, which occupied two days, took us through some of the most picturesque natural scenery to be found in the State, including Boonesboro, the scene of Daniel Boone's famous exploits with the Indians, at which place the entire brigade crossed the Kentucky River in a common scow which would hold only fifty men at a time. This delayed us for at least half a day, so that we had a good view of the wild surroundings.

I must here relate a personal incident. After arriving at Richmond, I was sent back to Winchester to bring forward some stores and supplies which had been necessarily left there. Our teams had not arrived from Covington, and I was detained for three days awaiting their appearance. I was stopping at the house of one Mr. Bush, a well-to-do planter, whose acquaintance I had made while the regiment was encamped there.

On the third night of my stay with him I was suddenly aroused from a sound sleep at one o'clock by two soldiers who had entered my room, and who immediately confronted me, one with a drawn sword, and the other with a revolver, which he held in one hand, and a lighted candle in the other. They said nothing, except to caution me that any attempt to move from my present position would be at the peril of my life. One of them commenced to search my clothes, while the other stood guard over me, holding his glistering revolver uncomfortably near my head.

I thought my hour had probably come, taking it for granted that the men were rebel soldiers and had taken advantage of my isolated situation to first rob and then dispatch me. But I finally mustered courage enough to ask them their business as politely as I knew how, and was promptly informed, greatly to my surprise, that I was a rebel spy and their prisoner and that they were Union soldiers sent there to arrest me. I at once felt relieved, knowing that I could readily establish my identity, and furthermore that I was tolerably safe anyway in the hands of Union soldiers.

Mr. Bush, who had followed them into the room in his night-clothes, immediately assured them that I was not a rebel spy, or even a rebel, but a member of the Twelfth Rhode Island Volunteers, and manifested considerable indignation that he should even be suspected of harboring rebel spies. Some papers and letters in my pockets supported the testimony of my host, and after considerable time spent in examining them, my brave (?) captors concluded that I was not the man they were looking for, and left me without so much as an apology for their mistake, to ponder upon my deceitful appearance. I learned the next day that two rebel spies had in fact been prowling about the neighborhood for several days, and that these officers (for such they were) had been searching for them.

A week at Richmond, three days at Paint Lick Creek, a tributary of the Cumberland, a week at Lancaster, and on we go, still southward, till we reach Crab Orchard, a Kentucky watering place of considerable note, where we remained for ten days. It was not every brigade that was allowed to spend this length of time at a fashionable southern watering place during the sultry days of June, at the expense of the government.

Instead of proceeding still further southward, as had been expected, we were here suddenly ordered to execute a "right about face," and retrace our steps to Nicholasville, a point twelve miles south of Lexington, where it was understood we were to take the cars en route for the far-off city of Vicksburg, where we were to assist General Grant in the siege against that rebel stronghold. This was not encouraging news to soldiers whose term of enlistment would expire in a little more than thirty days. Back we went, however, through the dust and heat, making the distance in two long days, the boys frequently rallying each other on the march with the remarks: "It's all in the nine months, boys;" and, "Why did you come for a soldier?"

Just as we got in sight of Nicholasville another surprise awaited us. One of the general's aids came dashing up to Colonel Browne with orders detaching his regiment from the brigade and directing him to report to General Carter at Somerset, more than seventy miles away, without delay. Half of this distance lay directly back over the route we had just travelled. This was, indeed, provoking. But we were soldiers, and had learned that our first and principal duty was prompt and unquestioning obedience to orders. So we bade goodbye to the other regiments of our brigade by giving three hearty cheers for each as they marched past us on their long journey to the West, and immediately turned our faces southward again and started for Somerset.

It then being nearly sunset, we bivouacked for the night as soon as we came to a convenient place, and resumed our backward march at daylight the next morning. The First Tennessee Battery and a regiment of mounted infantry soon joined us, and in company with them we reached Somerset, having gone by the way of Camp Dick Robinson and Hall's Gap, after a four days' march. In six successive days we had marched one hundred miles. And what was somewhat remarkable, we went into camp at the end of this time with not a man left behind.

After a stay of ten days at Somerset, during which time our base of supplies was at Stanford, thirty-three miles away, and could only be reached by our mule teams, we moved down to the Cumberland river, where we encamped on a high and precipitous bluff overlooking the river and the rugged mountainous scenery for a long distance. A brief rest and on, on we went again, bivouacking for a night on the battlefield of Mill Springs, where General Zollicoffer met his fate; climbing the mountains with our heavily laden mule teams, building bridges, constructing roads, and making but slow progress over the roughest country that I ever saw.

Several of my teams were capsized and rolled down a steep embankment, mules, drivers and all; others got mired in swamps, and it was with the greatest difficulty that they were ever extricated; but we pulled ourselves along in one way and another over a distance of thirty miles of this sort of country, and finally reached Jamestown (popularly known as "Jimtown"), on the southern border of Kentucky, on the twenty-third day of June, which place proved to be the end of our journey southward.

The Thirty-second Kentucky Infantry, called the "thirty two-sters," Colonel Wolford's famous cavalry regiment, six hundred strong,—the most dare-devil set of fellows, probably, in the Union service,—together with two mounted regiments of infantry, here reported to Colonel Browne and were temporarily placed under his command, and everything made ready for a brush with the rebels, which was daily expected, General Morgan being reported just in front of us with a large force.

On the twenty-ninth of June our pickets were suddenly attacked and driven in by the enemy, causing the greatest excitement in camp. The long roll was instantly sounded; the men rushed to their companies with all possible speed; the regiment was formed in line of battle at a double-quick by Lieutenant Colonel Shaw, and all was ready for the fray. Company A, Captain Alexander, and Company C, Captain Allen, had been previously stationed about half a mile in front, on a road leading south towards the Cumberland river, where they had felled trees and erected a sort of rude barricade called Fort Alexander, in honor of the captain in command, which position they continued to hold.

The battery took a position on the Columbus road, on which the enemy was approaching; the other regiments were just in the rear, while Wolford's cavalry went forward on a keen run, their famous commander being at least a hundred yards in front of his men when he passed our regiment, presenting, in connection with his headlong followers, a scene of the wildest excitement. He speedily came in contact with the enemy,—whose particular object at this time was the capture of our battery,—drove them back without bringing on a general engagement, captured a score or more of prisoners, and so thoroughly routed and scattered the enemy by his bold and vigorous dash, that they made no further attempt to dispute the possession of this antiquated town with our forces until the morning of the fourth of July following.

Our quartermaster's train, however, was attacked two days later, on its way from Green River, whither it had been for supplies, by a guerrilla band of about fifty men; but as the train was guarded by a company of mounted infantry from the Seventh Ohio, the attack was repulsed after a vigorous contest, with some loss on both sides, and our provisions and quartermaster arrived in camp unharmed the next day, to the great joy of the regiment, who were nearly out of supplies.

On the third of July a battle was fought near Lebanon, which was a short distance to the north of us, between a portion of

General Carter's forces and those under General Morgan,[1] in which quite a number were killed and several wounded.

We commenced the celebration of the glorious Fourth by forming in line of battle with alacrity at half-past three a. m., our pickets having been again driven in, and the rebels seeming determined to have a bout with us before we left Kentucky. And I think our men would as soon have fought as not on this occasion, being tired of the constant annoyance, and ready to prove to Kentucky bushwhackers what kind of stuff they were made of. But, fortunately for both sides doubtless, the rebels remained outside of "Jimtown," and our forces remained inside, resting on their arms all day, and momentarily expecting an attack, which, however, was not made.

And on the fifth of July, General Carter, deciding doubtless that this part of the State was not worth fighting for any longer, abandoned it to the enemy and moved his forces northward; first to Somerset, and then to Stanford, our base of supplies, which he continued to hold. Somerset was again reached after three days of the most difficult marching we had ever experienced, a heavy rain storm being in progress most of the time, rendering the movement of the artillery and heavy-laden army wagons well nigh impossible. With ten mules on one team, and two industrious swearers to drive them, I was only able to make a distance of two rods through the mire in the space of one whole hour, on one occasion during the first day of this march, which, by the way, was on Sunday.

Of course the army could move no faster than the wagon train on this march, as the rebels were immediately in our rear, ready to pounce upon us if a good opportunity was offered.

Eight days of continuous marching, most of the time over the same route we had travelled twice, and some of it three times before, and we were again at Nicholasville, where our regiment took the cars for Cincinnati by the way of Lexington. Our term of service had expired, but at the request of our greatly beloved General Burnside, we remained at Cincinnati for a week to as-

---

1. *History of Morgan's Cavalry* by Basil W. Duke also published by Leonaur.

sist in protecting that much frightened city from the raids of the somewhat ubiquitous General Morgan, who had preceded us from "Jimtown" to that more populous and inviting community. Another journey of a thousand miles—not, however, on foot—and the Twelfth Regiment was again at home.

Memorial of George H. Browne
Late Colonel of the Twelfth Regiment.

Colonel George H. Browne departed this life at Providence on the twenty-seventh day of September, *A. D.* 1885, in the sixty-eighth year of his age, sincerely lamented by all who knew him. He was a Rhode Islander by birth and education; thoroughly imbued with the history and traditions of the State, and always identified himself with its best interests. Conservative, candid and outspoken, and an excellent judge of human nature, he was not easily deceived or led to do an unwise or even an injudicious act. To say that he was a wise, prudent and thoroughly conscientious man, is but to voice the common sentiment of all those who knew him.

Since September of 1862, I have known Colonel Browne well, and been honored by his constant friendship. During the period of his service in the army, my duties brought me in almost daily contact with him; I was one of his mess during our Kentucky campaign, and had the opportunity to study his character and habits with deliberation; while since the war I have known him in the walks of private, professional and political life. And for stalwart manliness, transparent honesty and true nobility of character, I can unhesitatingly say that I have not known his superior.

As the commanding officer of the Twelfth Regiment, he at once inspired both the confidence and love of his men. His utmost energies were continually put forth for the efficiency and usefulness of his command, while his efforts for the personal welfare of each individual member thereof were proverbial. Indeed, in the latter respect he seemed more like a kind father watching over the welfare of his children, than a cold military commander issuing the stern edicts of war. It was his daily habit to go about the camp and personally inspect the same, frequently making his appearance in the tents and huts of the privates as well as in the quarters of the officers, for the purpose of ascertaining their condition as to cleanliness and comfort; inquiring after the wants of the men; visiting the hospital and speaking words of hope and good cheer to those who were sick, and in many other ways seeking to minister to the welfare of his command. A single instance of his unselfish devotion to the good of his men illustrates this characteristic.

On Sunday, May 3, 1863, his regiment marched from Richmond, Kentucky, to Paint Lick Creek, a distance of twelve miles, through a drenching rain. Many of the men had become footsore or otherwise disabled by reason of the great amount of marching they had recently done, and some of these became unable to complete the journey; whereupon, Colonel Browne, Lieutenant Colonel Shaw, and other field officers, gave up their horses to the use of these disabled ones, and themselves tramped with the men through the mud and rain for a good part of this distance.

Colonel Browne was a brave man. He faced the guns of the enemy at Fredericksburg where the battle waxed hottest, with as much apparent coolness as though simply facing his regiment on dress parade. A ball pierced his mantle; "the noise of battle hurtled in the air," and death-dealing missiles were flying thick about him, but he neither wavered nor blanched. Wherever his regiment was ordered to go, thither he promptly went in front of it, inspiring his followers with courage both by his genuine heroism and his manly words of cheer.

His bravery, however, was not of the ostentatious or noisy sort. It was more like the current of a still but deep-flowing river, which moves calmly but steadily onward, irresistibly drawing to itself, and unconsciously controlling all the lesser streams about it. He never paraded his virtues before his fellow-men, or posed as a hero or statesman for public applause. Indeed, he utterly scorned all attempts made by others for the sake of notoriety and position as vulgar and unworthy. He admired, however, and honestly won, the fame which follows generous and noble deeds, and not that which is sought after by the demagogue and the charlatan. He was notably considerate and courteous in his treatment of his subordinates in office, never seeming to command, while in fact exercising the most perfect control.

Colonel Browne retained an abiding interest in the men of his regiment to the day of his death. His greetings to them on the street, in the marts of trade, and especially at their annual reunions, were always warm and hearty. A single incident will serve to illustrate his interest in their welfare. Meeting me one day last winter on Westminster street, he said: "Judge, I've got some good news to tell you," and invited me to step into a bookstore which he was then passing while he should reveal it. "Do you remember Sergeant ——, of Company ——?" said he, his face all aglow with that expression of happiness which was peculiar to him.

"Yes, Colonel, I do; what about him?"

"Why, he's been out West, and by diligence and skill in a profitable business which he there engaged in, first as clerk and subsequently as one of the firm, and now as the manager thereof, has actually made his fortune, and is today a rich and highly respected man. And he came to see me the other day and told me all about it." And then with much enthusiasm and honest pride in his manner, said: "Isn't that good news from one of our boys?" Had this sergeant been his own son, he could hardly have manifested more joy in his prosperity.

His private benefactions to several of his men who had long been in indigent circumstances, are known and remembered by Him who said: "*Inasmuch as ye have done it unto one of the least of these my brethren, ye have done it unto me.*"

There was no circumlocution or ambiguity in Colonel Browne's methods. Whatever he had to do, he went about in

129

a direct and business-like way, and prosecuted it to completion in the same straightforward manner. He had none of the arts or tricks of the demagogue, and was utterly incapable of double-dealing or hypocrisy. And no man whom I have ever known, more thoroughly detested these base qualities in others. He had no patience with shams or subterfuges of any sort whatsoever, and did not hesitate to frown upon them with indignation whenever and wherever they appeared. If diplomacy has been correctly defined as being the art of concealing one's thoughts in his language, he never would have made a successful diplomat; for he always said just what he meant, and always meant just what he said.

Colonel Browne's abilities, both natural and acquired, were of a high order. He had a broad, vigorous and well-balanced mind, which had been thoroughly trained and disciplined to habits of logical and exact reasoning, and a power of analysis which led him to correct conclusions with almost mathematical certainty. He was not a superficial thinker, but always insisted on laying bare the very roots of the matter under consideration, and then gradually working upwards to natural and legitimate conclusions. His processes of reasoning were inductive rather than dogmatic. With such a mind, so constituted and developed, he was eminently fitted for positions of trust and responsibility, whether private or public, which foot the citizens both of his native town and State were not slow to learn and appreciate.

As a legislator he was diligent, prudent and conservative, possessing the courage of his convictions, always exerting a large and salutary influence by his candor, integrity and good judgment, and readily won the confidence and esteem of his associates. Public office was with him a public trust, to be administered with strictest fidelity and care.

In his chosen profession, in which the strength of his vigorous manhood was spent, he attained eminence and preferment, being a recognized leader of the bar of this State for many years before his death. A safe and able counsellor, an ingenuous and convincing advocate and an honorable opponent, he brought to the practice of his profession those qualities which insure success. Quibbles and quirks and barren technicalities were an abomination to him as a foundation upon which to base an action or a defense. Like Solon, "who built his commonweal on equity's wide base," so he built his legal structures on the broad principles of justice, truth and right.

In 1874 he was elected to the high and honorable office of Chief Justice of the Supreme Court of this State by a legislature composed mainly of his political opponents, a monumental tribute to his integrity, learning and ability. He declined the office, however, and remained in the profession which he had dignified and honored to the day of his death.

As a private citizen he was a man of unimpeachable character, generous impulses, and high and noble purposes. His life was pure and unostentatious, and his manner frank and undisguised. Let us ever cherish his memory, and strive to emulate his virtues.

ALSO FROM LEONAUR

AN APACHE CAMPAIGN IN THE SIERRA MADRE by *John G. Bourke*—An Account of the Expedition in Pursuit of the Chiricahua Apaches in Arizona, 1883.

BILLY DIXON & ADOBE WALLS by *Billy Dixon and Edward Campbell Little*—Scout, Plainsman & Buffalo Hunter, *Life and Adventures of "Billy" Dixon* by Billy Dixon and *The Battle of Adobe Walls* by Edward Campbell Little (*Pearson's Magazine*).

WITH THE CALIFORNIA COLUMN by *George H. Petis*—Against Confederates and Hostile Indians During the American Civil War on the South Western Frontier, *The California Column, Frontier Service During the Rebellion* and *Kit Carson's Fight With the Comanche and Kiowa Indians*.

THRILLING DAYS IN ARMY LIFE by *George Alexander Forsyth*—Experiences of the Beecher's Island Battle 1868, the Apache Campaign of 1882, and the American Civil War.

INDIAN FIGHTS AND FIGHTERS by *Cyrus Townsend Brady*—Indian Fights and Fighters of the American Western Frontier of the 19th Century.

THE NEZ PERCÉ CAMPAIGN, 1877 by *G. O. Shields & Edmond Stephen Meany*—Two Accounts of Chief Joseph and the Defeat of the Nez Percé, *The Battle of Big Hole* by G. O. Shields and *Chief Joseph, the Nez Percé* by Edmond Stephen Meany.

CAPTAIN JEFF OF THE TEXAS RANGERS by *W. J. Maltby*—Fighting Comanche & Kiowa Indians on the South Western Frontier 1863-1874.

SHERIDAN'S TROOPERS ON THE BORDERS by *De Benneville Randolph Keim*—The Winter Campaign of the U. S. Army Against the Indian Tribes of the Southern Plains, 1868-9.

WILD LIFE IN THE FAR WEST by *James Hobbs*—The Adventures of a Hunter, Trapper, Guide, Prospector and Soldier.

THE OLD SANTA FE TRAIL by *Henry Inman*—The Story of a Great Highway.

LIFE IN THE FAR WEST by *George F. Ruxton*—The Experiences of a British Officer in America and Mexico During the 1840's.

ADVENTURES IN MEXICO AND THE ROCKY MOUNTAINS by *George F. Ruxton*—Experiences of Mexico and the South West During the 1840's.

LEONAUR

ALSO FROM LEONAUR
AVAILABLE IN SOFTCOVER OR HARDCOVER WITH DUST JACKET

FARAWAY CAMPAIGN *by F. James*—Experiences of an Indian Army Cavalry Officer in Persia & Russia During the Great War.

REVOLT IN THE DESERT *by T. E. Lawrence*—An account of the experiences of one remarkable British officer's war from his own perspective.

MACHINE-GUN SQUADRON *by A. M. G.*—The 20th Machine Gunners from British Yeomanry Regiments in the Middle East Campaign of the First World War.

A GUNNER'S CRUSADE *by Antony Bluett*—The Campaign in the Desert, Palestine & Syria as Experienced by the Honourable Artillery Company During the Great War .

DESPATCH RIDER *by W. H. L. Watson*—The Experiences of a British Army Motorcycle Despatch Rider During the Opening Battles of the Great War in Europe.

TIGERS ALONG THE TIGRIS *by E. J. Thompson*—The Leicestershire Regiment in Mesopotamia During the First World War.

HEARTS & DRAGONS *by Charles R. M. F. Crutwell*—The 4th Royal Berkshire Regiment in France and Italy During the Great War, 1914-1918.

INFANTRY BRIGADE: 1914 *by John Ward*—The Diary of a Commander of the 15th Infantry Brigade, 5th Division, British Army, During the Retreat from Mons.

DOING OUR 'BIT' *by Ian Hay*—Two Classic Accounts of the Men of Kitchener's 'New Army' During the Great War including *The First 100,000* & *All In It*.

AN EYE IN THE STORM *by Arthur Ruhl*—An American War Correspondent's Experiences of the First World War from the Western Front to Gallipoli-and Beyond.

STAND & FALL *by Joe Cassells*—With the Middlesex Regiment Against the Bolsheviks 1918-19.

RIFLEMAN MACGILL'S WAR *by Patrick MacGill*—A Soldier of the London Irish During the Great War in Europe including *The Amateur Army*, *The Red Horizon* & *The Great Push*.

WITH THE GUNS *by C. A. Rose & Hugh Dalton*—Two First Hand Accounts of British Gunners at War in Europe During World War 1- Three Years in France with the Guns and With the British Guns in Italy.

THE BUSH WAR DOCTOR *by Robert V. Dolbey*—The Experiences of a British Army Doctor During the East African Campaign of the First World War.